The
ORIGIN
of
Opportunity

The
ORIGIN
of
Opportunity

Reality's Dirty Secret...
Unleash the Power of "Nothing"
Be Free of Financial and Mental Restraints

ANDREW CARTWRIGHT

NEXT CENTURY
PUBLISHING

If you've picked up this book you're probably wondering what is the *Origin of Opportunity*? Thousands of self-help book authors have published their recipes for success, love, money, happiness, health. Theirs is simple cookie-cutter approach, a five-step program, or a step-by-step formula for…. Now I ask you: Are any of those programs working for you? Are you like everyone else? No. You are unique! You are an individual and authentic. I'm just like you, but I discovered reality's dirty secrets and the true power of unleashing "nothing." This book will take you on a journey that will completely blow your mind, rock your emotions to the core and set you free, financially, mentally, and emotionally. I will show you the *Origin of the Opportunity*, and destroy your reality so you can have a new reality that isn't based on what others say or what you have been told.

This is how my journey started.

When I was 12 years old, my stepfather was waiting in the living room, after I came home from school. He looked very angry and he grabbed my arm and hauled me up to my bedroom. He then sat me down on my bed and began yelling at me. "At 12 years old I was on the streets making my own way, now you will have to learn as I did. Starting today and going forward you will not ask your mother or me for money." This event set the course of my destiny and changed my life forever. From that moment, I had to figure out how to get lunch money, a bike, and anything I wanted on my own. I had the good fortune of some relief at Christmas and my birthday. These times were overflowing with abundant gifts, followed by 363 days of fear, loss, and scarcity. That same year, I started to work at the cafeteria at school 6 am, serving breakfast and lunch. I was paid in food for working there. I earned more food than I could eat, so every lunchtime I shared it with eight other people who could not afford to buy food, and wouldn't or didn't work for it. As you could imagine I instantly had "friends." Soon after, I started my first business.

Imagine a time when you were into a situation you never anticipated. I'm sure you became very resourceful as you faced your reality. You did not have a choice, and out of necessity your rose to the challenge and had to deliver. Throughout this book, I'm going to put that ability at your fingertips, to be able to push that button at your will. Nothing will be out of your reach.

Here's to "nothing"!

Andrew

Origin of Opportunity
Reality's Dirty Secret...Unleash the Power of "Nothing," Be Free of Financial and Mental Restraints

Austin, TX
www.NextCenturyPublishing.com

ISBN: 978-1-68102-640-4

Printed in the United States of America

CONTENTS

Part One
UNLOCK YOUR POSSIBILITY

Part Two
YOUR STORY AND MINE—WHAT'S THE CAUSE WE ARE TRYING TO EFFECT?

Part Three
THE REALM

Part Four
POSSIBILITY IN PRACTICE

Part Five
YOUR TURN

The ORIGIN of Opportunity

PREFACE

Origin of Opportunity is a book that expands and improves the quality of our life. By using life's experiences, I have created the recipe that has made me extremely successful and that I will be sharing with you. This recipe will allow you to have the wealth, happiness, and health you always dreamed of. You will be able to make more money via creating companies, relationships, and opportunities from nothing. You will enjoy the value of having peace of mind as well as be able to escape the trap of meaning that is destroying your potential. You will conquer, and win over the daily negative thoughts patterns of the mind. **This will end mental and emotional suffering forever.** You will find your inner *wise being,* that you may be ignoring now, and get your questions answered.

This book is about remembering, questioning, and reexamining our currently imposed limitations. If you have ever been around a three-year-old, you know there is no such thing as homeland security. In fact, they are truly a domestic, household terrorist. They do whatever they want, with whatever they

It will end mental and emotional suffering forever.

1

can get their hands on, with no regard for how we commonly use that "thing." Communicating with them about what not to do is completely pointless—in one ear and out the other—before you can finish talking and then they're back at it again. There's no limitation or restriction present, and they are truly in the moment emotionally and mentally. By reading my book, you can get back to this true freedom. **The state of zero. Your origin**.

These solutions captured in my book are universal and can be applied to all areas of life: work, relationships, health and others. Immerse yourself in this book and come with me on a challenging journey exposing your origin. You will be introduced to new viewpoints and truths that will open you up to discover your authentic self. You'll be confronted by questions about meaning, worth, purpose, value, money, reality, time, language, mental mindsets, and limitations. You'll discover what you think your identity is and create the opportunity to uncover your infinite self.

What I will be sharing with you I've used to create opportunities day after day, year after year for over thirty-two years. I want to help everyone I can to be wealthy, healthy, and happy. I have the blueprint for success in business and life. I have originated many success-ful companies and relationships with ease. I have imagined, purchased, created, en-titled, built, and sold several mega man-sions, houses, restaurants, night clubs, industrial buildings, and even a shipping terminal building. I hold several professional licenses as a real estate broker, insurance agent, car dealer, a finance and leasing company principal. I compete in several Ironman races, marathons, and car races. I am a certified race car driver, skydiver, and scuba diver. I was a poster boy all over the world for Microsoft Office 2000. I have acted in movies, TV,

**The state of zero.
Your origin.**

and theater and I am in the Screen Actors Guild.

I had the pleasure of acting with Robin Williams, a famous American actor whom I have incredible respect for and feel blessed to have been in three movies with: *What Dreams May Come, Patch Adams,* and *Bicentennial Man.* Williams was one of the most personable human beings I have ever met. I spent 10 to 13 hours a day with him. His mind was unbelievably fast and sharp. He was in the moment with me completely. He revealed to me so much of his suffering and his understanding of media, the reality of our pop culture, and his insider views on the truth about people. As we were waiting for the camera crew to set up we looked through magazines, and he explained to me the purpose for stories about famous Hollywood celebrities, like who they really are compared to their images and branded identities because he knew them personally.

I experienced much of the same while acting, but I love the work and all the great conversations we had on set. I want to thank the following people for their honest, vulnerable, and revealing conversations: George Lucus, Philip Seymour Hoffman, Cameron Diaz, Diane Keaton, Chris O'Donnell, Renee Zellweger, Cuba Gooding Jr, Max von Sydow, Don Johnson, Cheech Marin, Jeff Perry, Jaime Gomez, Yasmine Bleeth, Kelly Hu, Reene Zagware, Daniel Roebuck, James Cromwell, James Gammon, Devon Sawa and many more. I would also like to thank the movie producers who made me a part of *What Dreams May Come, Patch Adams, The Other Sister, The Bachelor, Around the Fire, Breaking Out,* TV's *Nash Bridges* for three years, and *Party of Five.* I want to thank Microsoft for choosing me as a poster boy for Office 2000. But most importantly I am thankful for the inspiration of the amazing woman, Anna Zakowska, whom I am madly in love with who supports my dreams.

Introduction

My goal for this book is that you can overcome the obstacle of your identity and concepts of yourself—the rules and limitations you've set for yourself. Over time, these limitations in your mind are embedded with concepts of loss, which started to build fences around your life for protection. Life surrenders any vitality because of the losses we've suffered in love, in business, in finance, in friendship, and in the world. Your fear of loss provides the building blocks for your jar, one that doesn't contain the ability to experience truly your origin, the authentic self. **By allowing yourself to forget who you've been, so you can become who you are.**

This book will not give you handy strategies, tactics, or solutions to embrace and live by like our culture of simple sound bites that require no thinking. That would only keep you from experiencing the moment, vitality, and any true authenticity. What we hope to explore in this book is completely different than simple, handy clever strategies, tactics and answers that once known will no longer serve any real purpose. You can find the information on the Internet and obtain easy answers on Google, Yahoo, Twitter, Facebook or Bing.

Through this book there is a real possibility you could find your true origin—not the "self" you make up for people and tell yourself you are. In the process you can experience true discovery. The hard part is that most material today will just tell you what to believe and they won't show you how to process things to find true answers. You will have to look inside yourself to truly see for yourself. I can't do that for you. You will have to be your witness, jury, and judge.

As you keep that in mind, I want to offer a warning about what you are about to read. It may offend you and frustrate you. Starting with language. What is language but an amazing, useful tool that we often don't even consider or look at for what it is comprised of? Consider the symbols—letters—arbitrarily organized into words that will evoke concepts in your imagination and mental image, sound and feeling library—ideas that you have in mind. What I want you to realize is that those experiences have devolved into memories, and those memories have developed into concepts. Just as the word "success" only represents actual success, your concepts are arbitrary associations from events you feel represent success and your association to it in language. The POWER OF WORDS is in what you just read. You created them. You can *re*create them. You gave them the meaning. You can recreate your meaning. You don't have to get stuck in the past unless you choose to. As Albert Einstein said:

Find your true origin not the "self" you make up.

> *"Reality is merely an illusion, albeit a very persistent one."*

Consider this: **Racism doesn't exist**. It's crazy to think the dictionary has racism as a noun. It's not a noun. I say racism is a verb. We have to be carefully taught it's not natural. We made and make it up. I know most people will reject this statement and that's okay. I expect you to initially. If you truly embrace this moment in time, the now only exists. You would have to come out of the now and remember something, label that as racism or create in this moment the concept of racism or have an image of racism in the future. But racism itself doesn't exist unless we make it so. It's simply a concept. In any given moment we can only put it there or bring it up. It's used and is being used as a concept. Consider this: **Tuesday doesn't exist**; we make it up, agree on it together and that the agreement is reality. Is it really? Or just a group agreement. Look past that, you find we make up religion, sexism, culture and the list goes on. Then we get stuck in them, fight to defend or enforce these concepts. **What can you say really exists?** When you really confront that question, watch the weight of the past and future fall off your shoulders opening up new opportunities that now become visible. Look at this moment now, what can you prove exists? When you operate from your true origin, life will completely open up. Think you have the power to make up your own life? So if racism, sexism and Tuesday is working for you, at least you have the power to realize you are making it up, thereby originating and creating it. They're your powerful or powerless conceptual ORIGINATIONS. You chose!

Interesting fact. It's been forty-seven years since interracial marriage was given the green light. That being said, **Racism doesn't exist.** what does the U.S. marital landscape look like now? Well, let's take a look at interracial couples in America today by the numbers? Today 87 percent of Americans approve of whites and blacks tying the knot, according to Gallup. Compare this to 1959 when a measly 4 percent approved!

The Pew study found that nearly 40 percent of married people who tied the knot since 2010 have a spouse who identifies with a different religion than they do (compared to the 19 percent who married before 1960).

If you learn anything from this book, it won't be because I told you. There's nothing here that you don't already know. You just may not realize it. Also, there may be times when you could feel personally attacked for your thoughts and life choices. It's not my intent to judge or be *right* about you or anyone else. This book is not about me being *right*. It's about *you* living, loving, and enjoying life to the fullest organic state while continuing to learn from your current experiences. I feel very passionate about living life to the fullest and continuing to grow and learn.

What can you say really exists?

This learning requires us to open up space— beyond the jar—to understand things and a lot of these concepts that you're going to read may not be concepts you can grasp immediately, yet that doesn't mean they may not be true. Because what will be communicated throughout this book is the truth for me and a lot of people I've worked with. I'll communicate my truth or as close as I can get to it now. The real power comes from you being able to take and generate your truth.

I hope to inspire and evoke your origin, the "real you," so you can be guided out exposed in your path to experience life fully. You don't have to hide anymore—as I did and many do for years—locked up in concepts, beliefs, ideas and images not our own. We walk around life trading concepts with other people who, in turn, living in their "box," traded their concepts with ours. We stop truly living when we live in concepts, loved through concepts, and developed our being through concepts that are not of our creation. My hope for you is that you can experience family, friends, love, ecstasy, success, vitality, commitment, dependability, and responsibility in life in a story of *your* choosing. I pray you can create the context of your life so that you can generate what you're searching for and the self, your origin, that authentically can come forth and give yourself a full life and an uninterrupted flow toward the success or whatever it is you seek in your life.

Consider that anything we identify with sets us up for the only available options that support that identification and that identity. So why might we find some concepts hard to grasp? It is because they don't fit in the box that we have, a set of options that we operate from to support what we have identified with that now have slipped in and became part of our identity.

Just because it does not make sense to us doesn't necessarily mean that it isn't true, and it can't create enormous value for us. If we stay open for learning long enough, we can understand new ideas. By being open to the possibility, you can allow yourself to think about a concept in a new way, one that brings a broader understanding than if you tried to force it into your existing set of options or reject it because it's not serving you in the way you expected.

After all, there will be a lot in life we don't understand, and yet there can be a tremendous value that we can get by taking a look at it, being with it, and opening ourselves up to the possibility of the value that it could create in our lives. I wish you all the best on this adventure and exploration of what's possible for you. You will be shown the traps that keep you from getting what you want. When life brings you to your knees, you never let it take you out of the game.

Consider that anything we identify with sets us up for the only available options that support that identification and that identity.

Part One

UNLOCK YOUR POSSIBILITY

CHAPTER 1

Break Out of the Glass Jar and Let the Fleas Loose

Are we much different than a flea? Do we share similar behaviors? Do we have more capabilities than a flea? Maybe.

But maybe not. Check this out.

A flea can jump forty-nine times its body length. A six-foot-tall person would have to be able to jump 295 feet long or 16 stories (160 feet) straight up to match that. A flea can be submerged in water for 18-20 hours and still live. Imagine that.

A flea will put limits on itself without even realizing its circumstances have changed. Put a flea in a jar without a lid, and it'll hop right out. But **How do we limit ourselves this same way?** put the lid on the jar, and after three days of head-banging attempts, the flea will never leap higher than just below the lid. Even if you remove the lid, the flea won't jump any higher than its now self-imposed limit. Never realizing that circumstances have changed. Even worse, neither will flea's 5,000 offspring.

How do we limit ourselves this same way? What lids have we hit? What lids are we not even aware of? Even though the flea has the strength and ability to jump out of the jar, it doesn't. It continues to jump only up to where it almost hit the lid. Eventually, the fleas will all die in that jar. How have we calibrated our lives to live within boundaries that don't exist, but remain in our minds as true or real? But if a new non-programmed flea is introduced to the jar full of programmed fleas, they can follow the lead of the rebel and emerge into freedom. I am that new flea. Life outside the jar is amazing.

Time to Recalibrate Your Life and eliminate our Internal and External Parasites

Take a quick look at these simple questions to examine a sample of our limitations.

What can or can't you do?

What would or wouldn't you do?

What should or shouldn't you do?

What could or couldn't you do?

What must or mustn't you do?

What are or aren't you able to do?

Who set these limits?

Why did they set these limits?

How could they set these limits?

Why would they set these limits?

Let's explore all the **possibilities**.

Let's leap out of our jars! Circumstances have now changed!

CHAPTER 2

Free Yourself; Reality is an Opinion

Socrates, one of the greatest philosophers of all time, was killed for what I am about to share with you. Countries, leaders, and lawmakers don't want you to understand what I am going to make plain. This information undermines the methods, strategies, and tactics used by the gurus and authorities alike, reducing their influence and power over you; they will *not* want you to read this book. This information in the wrong hands has already destroyed great nations and killed many people. In the right hands, it can and does transform reality.

Your reality is just your opinion of what you think is real.

Your reality, a group enforced agreement, is forged by a culture interested more in telling you what to believe rather than how to think and what to question! There are more physical places and people teaching you what your beliefs should be than there are places and people teaching you how to open up thinking, feeling, imagination, and question for yourself to expose your origin.

Your reality is just your opinion of what you think is real. What is reality? What is real? How do we know it's real? Is what we think real? Is what we feel real?

When we are born, we are thrown into a rushing river of life's current conversation. We start to mimic the language of our parents who **speak into us** that which becomes our language with invented definitions, made up definitions and assumed definitions by the context of what words mean—all before we even open a dictionary or any reference material. Talking before we even enter school, having absorbed all their words, expressions, beliefs, options, limits, possibilities, rules, guides for living and their concepts about life. We can't help but get these limited and made up viewpoints, because they're all that are offered to us through our exposure.

We absorb the programming from our environment. According to science, our identity is mostly formed by age eight. Although never completed, it is a psychological structure and also a complex subject of contemporary humanitarian science. These programs are buried in our subconscious program or narrative. For example, programs like, "You dirty rotting good for nothing, you will never amount to anything. You were a mistake, wish we never had you. You're going to be a criminal, you're going to be a prisoner. You're going to end up dead or in jail, and no one's life is better because you exist."

Imagine at age two we understand and use about 300 words. By age five we are conversational with a vocabulary of 5000 words before even one day of school, and without opening a dictionary to look up a single meaning of a word. The meanings of the words we use are the result of the language that surrounds us and our approximation of what we understand the words to be. Life is told to us with absoluteness: "These are your parents, and this is your home where you are to come back to every night or be in serious trouble. You have to wear clothes. Here is your family: this is your cousin, your weird uncle, and here is your cranky aunt. This is your school, yes; you have to go and

YOU'VE BECOME A SLAVE TO YOUR STORY! A slave to your own self-importance or even worse someone else's.

don't ask why. This is what a friend is, and here are the available friends you have access to with your limited reach. This is your teacher; listen to him because he knows things you need to know. We live in this town, in this state, in this country, and we act like this because we are___ and we are from____. Our family gains weight easy. We are unlucky. You don't listen. You'll never be rich. You have no talent. You're tone deaf. We are Greeks and Greeks don't do this ____ and that ____. Your personal story is, and our family story is."

What is embedded in the person is now clouding and becoming their identifying characteristics/story. It is now bigger than who they are: "I'm stubborn, I'm fat, I'm Greek, Asian, Black...on and on it goes. This is IT (the story is now bigger than you) and "IT" has taken over.

You have become a slave to your story! A slave to your own self-importance or even worse someone else's. A completely internal parasite. Consider how much you have invested into your story. Consider how much other people have invested in your story.

Your personal internal dictator and ruler. King "IT"

That you, now becomes this story, and the story becomes something that you are, and that something that you now identify with as you, which I will call "IT." Your personal internal dictator and ruler. King "IT" is completely invisible to most people. And on IT goes the story of "you." Your story "IT" has now taken over you. This is now you! And IT is you. You must defend IT! Who is IT? What does IT want? Where is IT going? What is IT up to? What is IT hiding? What is IT pretending to know? When did IT take over? Is IT you or are you IT? "IT" can be quite confusing because you no longer see the separation between you and IT. You can become liberated from King IT and see past your stories of who you say you are. Operate from your origin.

You come to accept that you just are, and IT just is.

Everyone has on their own King "IT" set of rules, which is the jar. From the beginning, you are given the only available options that keep you from upsetting the jar and the kingdom of everyone around you with your fixed mold until you reach a point that you don't know their options, jars, and molds from your origin. You come to accept that you just **are,** and IT just **is.** You don't see a difference between "IT" and **you.** Your origin doesn't get noticed by IT which sets up your set of responses which becomes automatic, autopilot, and safe inside the Kingdom or your jar. IT is a tiny molecule compared to your origin. You can only give your power to IT. IT can't take your power from you.

How is IT controlling your life without you knowing? How do you even see what you are not even aware of? How do you go somewhere you don't even know? How can you be what you don't even know you could be? You could say you are blind to IT. Now is the time to shine the light on IT and open the areas of your being and livingness to discover what's *really possible.*

IT is a tiny molecule compared to your origin.

You can and will be set free if you're willing. Stay with me, and let's take this ride together and boldly, bravely, openly depart from the currently unknowable unknown. Like a black hole, when your limitations orbit around the gravitational pull of possibility, those limitations will collapse into nothingness as well. Even though you can't see, matter orbits around an apparently empty space and gives evidence of the existences of things completely unseen, unreal, and unheard. Yet when the matter gets too close, suddenly its existence to you is no more, apparently collapsing into nothingness. Like a black hole, when your limitations orbit around the gravitational pull of possibility, those limitations will collapse into nothingness as well. A little practice with the power of possibility and limitations won't have much of a chance and everything you ever could imagine becomes possible.

Like a black hole, when your limitations orbit around the gravitational pull of possibility, those limitations will collapse into nothingness as well.

CHAPTER 3

Your Stories Determine Your Outcome

Why are you not getting what you want? What is going wrong, or what are you not doing when you don't get what you want? What would you have to give up to get what you want? Who would you have to *be* to get what you want? Who and what are your internal and external parasites?

After all, your life is your story to tell and choose to share with the world. With billions of things happening, listen to how you might start your story... What happened to me... Why isn't it happening the way you want?

Your stories—the ones you're *living*, not the one you *want*—are what you brought here to this time and place. You could have brought many stories from anywhere, anytime, anything. Why this one? Why now? Your conversation, your stories shape your outcome and your reality. Might you just be stuck in bad stories? You practice and tell stories to people and yourself to impress upon yourself what you want people and yourself to feel and think about you.

Can you handle the truth about yourself? We are going to peel back the layers of the onion, of those stories you've made up just to "be right," just so IT (your story) can survive. We are going to peel off layer, upon layer, upon layer of these stories to justify IT: why you're late; why you don't have the relationships you want; why you don't have the business you want; and the list goes on. All the *whys* are the stories you have built the onion with, the deep inside of which is the core of you, now completely unrecognizable and unreachable. Your authentic self has been lost and covered up. Story, after story, after story. Layer upon layer.

Your stories are covering up the real, authentic you, your origin.

Well, don't you? Because when people buy your stories, you're really off the hook. You no longer have to be responsible because you've got a "good" reason. You've got a "great" excuse. You've got a "solid" justification for why you're not getting what you want, and you need them to buy these stories because it's pretty embarrassing that you don't have what you want. It's sad you don't have what you want. It's uncomfortable not to have what you want. It can be hard to keep up the stories that go on and those that are going on. Those stories are exhausting and sabotaging you. They are working against you.

Your stories are covering up the real, authentic you, your origin.

Oh, I know you can make up very clever stories. I did it myself. Stories that can be very dramatic, emotional, and carefully justified and practiced on hundreds, maybe thousands, of people. I recognize your stories because I've told my share of reasonable, excuse-driven backstories—where I am from, who I think I am, why I'm this and that, my name, my parents. I put out those stories to someone to get them to "buy" my narrative. Many people bought my story, and I bought my story too. But when people didn't buy my carefully thought out, crafted, and justified story, I would get quite upset. Maybe not even talk to them again...

This is not who you are. These stories are the excuses based on the past; they don't exist in the here and now. Why do you think it takes so much out of you to maintain your stories? Here is the truth: What exists at this moment is *your choice*: an opportunity to create, to invent and reinvent yourself. Your stories come with limitations, and when you believe those stories, they will jar you in, setting up limitations on your life and rules by which you *must* behave. You live with folks who've bought all your stories, and they now expect you to act in a certain way. The stories that you identify with created the only available options that support the existence of stories of people around you in the first place.

> **Because when people buy your stories, you're really off the hook.**

It's a self-serving prophecy; their stories create a vicious circle to be right about being right.

Then you meet someone brand new who offers you different stories, you get a completely blank canvas to create whoever story of who you are. They may just look at you and say, "Wow, that's different. I don't understand why he told me that story, yet that's okay." Now you're committed to that story, and you insist until they submit, "Well, okay. I guess I can understand that." They know you're

> **What exists at this moment is your choice: an opportunity to create, to invent and reinvent yourself.**

selling your story, but they buy it because they're in their jars too, lining you up to sell their own stories to you. We buy each other's stories, reasons, excuses, and justifications because we truly believe we like the jar we're in, because it feels comfortable, and we think it's comforting.

However, the truth behind creating the stories is uncomfortable. Losing is uncomfortable. Handling and dealing with the truth is uncomfortable. It's uncomfortable that you fail out of a relationship. It's uncomfortable that you cheated and got cheated on. It's uncomfortable that you broke your promises. It's uncomfortable that you broke your agreements knowingly. In fact, it's more than uncomfortable. It's downright embarrassing and even sometimes terrifying. To have the most positive and pleasurable experience in life, you think you must confine yourself to a jar that doesn't have you at risk of losing. And that's sad. You surrender to the loss by making up stories, justifications, excuses, and reasons to cover it up. You start making up stories.

You put yourself into a jar with limited options and no possibility of more. You think and feel this is safe enough so that you're not stuck living in fear. You're very safe in that jar: you know how it works, you've become mentally domesticated. You don't get sad or angry, and you are afraid of being happy. After all, maybe you see happy people get attacked just because they are, in fact, happy. That's the strange thing: people are going to attack happy people, so you don't allow yourself to be happy. You play it safe in your jar.

Over time you become smaller and smaller, but the world becomes bigger and bigger. It gets harder and more frustrating to live in your jar, even if you don't admit it. You settle for a jarred-in life. That jar is sabotaging the original, authentic, and realest you that's possible, unreasonable, inexcusable, unjustifiable, unbelievable, limitless—the true you. Because of the jar, the true you is covered up, and you walk around as if you're a living dead person. You're safe, yet you don't get to live authentically. In fact, you don't even know what authentic is anymore. You don't know who you are. Even your

That jar is sabotaging the original, authentic, and realest you that's possible, unreasonable, inexcusable, unjustifiable, unbelievable, limitless—the true you.

clothing decisions are based on your fear of looking bad or not being fashion right. You're acting and behaving based on your losses. You're living out of your losses and in fear because of them. In a jar that you're safe with... that's where you live.

"Are you telling your story, or is your story telling you?" You're not living. You're dead, passing by life, with your jar getting smaller and smaller, until someday, hopefully, it's all over. As you get older, you're looking forward to the fact that it will all be over soon because you're suffering from this misery. You suffer through life.

You tell yourself, "Oh yeah, but you've got tactics. You've got the strategy. You've got philosophy. You've got all kinds of handy information, answers, and statistics." You aren't living. When you're living within somebody else's context of strategy and philosophy, you're not living your true authentic self. So my question for you is, "Are you telling your story, or is your story telling you?"

One more time, pay attention:

ARE YOU TELLING YOUR STORY...OR IS YOUR
STORY TELLING YOU?

CHAPTER 4

Who Voted on Your Quality of Life?

Let's start with your quality of life. Consider this as a possibility: Your quality of life has nothing to do with the circumstances out of which you've come or events that have happened in your life or anything else that has led up to where you are now.

Think about that for a moment.

This is a concept many people have a hard time understanding because of the stories and excuses they've made throughout their lives, yet it's true.

I can hear the excuses already. Right now, you can't even consider this as a possibility, that you can choose your quality of life because you are going to want to be right, your stories must be right, because of the circumstances of who you are and how you got here. Those circumstances and events have shaped your life, and they demand that the quality of your life has to be a certain way. **The true quality of your life is determined by you, and it is a choice.** The true quality of your life is determined by you, and it is a choice. A different possibility, say a possibility that didn't come from your thoughts, didn't come from your past, didn't come from a past projection into the future, yet was organic—originated from possibility. This space, this opening, and the quality of your life were not necessarily determined by the circumstances or events of your past or even your projected fears of what you think may or actually could, happen in the future.

I want you to consider that as a possibility, not as the truth, not as I want you to believe it, yet just consider it as a possibility.

CHAPTER 5

Let's Get Our Minds Dirty

Are you successful? Oh, the possibilities. "Success" is one of the most misunderstood words we have, and yet it is the unspecified aim of the average person. They want it; they just may not know what it looks like.

First, I want to acknowledge that you are already successful. You have come a long way. As human beings, we have all come a long way, and we are all very successful. Our forefathers could not have imagined the life we have today as a nation and as a world, as we have done amazing things. Some of our biggest achievements are daily occurrences that go almost unnoticed or unappreciated. As a nation, we have been to space many times with NASA—and now private companies are even entering space on their own. A child can edit movies and soundtracks from a computer that can be purchased for a few hundred dollars. Many diseases of the past are now nonexistent. Farm work that once took hundreds of people now requires just a few people using machines. Think about writing a letter, putting a stamp on it, putting it in the mailbox, and waiting for a reply. I can't even remember the last time I did that. Now we write a letter, push a button, and it reaches the recipient in seconds.

I am writing this book to a person I consider to be already very successful: you. I think you are already complete and worthy of what life offers you and the gifts you possess inside. Has anyone ever told you that? By picking up this book, you've acknowledged that you're looking for something more. This is in itself a gift you have given yourself. This book is an opportunity to receive new gifts in a profound way and open you up to more than you have been seeing. I know that you live in a society that can be critical, cold, and distant. This is about you tapping into the infinite within you.

You need to start by asking a few simple questions: Who am I now? Who do I want to become? What do I want to become?

It's my nature to adopt an entrepreneurial approach of looking at things, and that approach is about creation. What do you want to create? Even if it's creating a job, the fact that you're creating that job means you're taking responsibility for the duties you've taken on. You have a responsibility for acting in the best interest of those items or things you've taken responsibility for.

Forget about the company. Forget about everything. Forget about all the static and drama, and focus on what have you taken responsibility for. What area? What are you supposed to produce in that section? What are the results that will keep that section surviving? How do you improve that section and grow it?

These are questions that help you look at life from an entrepreneurial discovery perspective. By taking this approach to address different aspects of your life, a question arises: "Is there a path, a gentler path, a better path, one that's not as difficult, not littered with losses?"

By answering that question, you create the value that you see and want for yourself. You will begin to look honestly at your reality and your ability to question your current life. In doing so you allow the stream of possibilities to rush in. You discover and acquire insights that have solidly impacted your life, which will empower you to improve the quality of your life personally and professionally. By developing your "Philosophy of Possibility," you develop a new vision for your life—a vision that is free of jars built by the past, by concepts grown from loss.

Break out of the trance and live the life you dream about, now.

The truth about you is revealed in and through your words and actions. Most books, talks, lectures, and theories about philosophy and life are passive. The Philosophy of Possibility is not, nor is this book. To experience the Philosophy of Possibility and have it be revealed to you in your daily life will take some practice. In your adult life, you may be able to go along in an almost trancelike state of predictable patterns not knowing one day from the next, but it's time to break that monotony. Break out of the trance and live the life you dream about, *now*.

You can start the process by taking one sheet of paper and writing down what you'd like your life to look like. What *is* that life you've been dreaming about? What's missing from your life now that would make that dream happen?

On the back of the page, write down three things:

- What is stopping you from having the life you see?

- What are the payoffs for you being right about this?

- What are you missing out on as a result of accepting the payoffs?

Finally, write exactly what you want to get out of this book and how you hope it will impact your life. The impact of communication depends on starting out with an honest and authentic relationship. My goal is that you will get exactly what you hope for.

Part Two

YOUR STORY AND MINE—WHAT'S
THE CAUSE WE ARE TRYING TO
EFFECT?

CHAPTER 6

Who Cares Who You Are or Who I Am?

Who am I? That's an interesting and difficult question for all of us. We take this question in our current culture and use handy generic answers that people accept as true. Have you ever asked yourself, **"Who am I? Really, who am I?"**

My name is Andrew Eddie Cartwright. Is that who I am? No. That is only my name. There are many people in the world with the same name. My name can't truly define or confine me. In fact, I gave myself that name when I was eighteen years old. My given name at birth was Eddie Carrol Cartwright: Eddie after the paperboy my mom thought was sweet, Carrol after my grandfather, and Cartwright, our family name. I guess my parents then were searching to have the meaning in my name. My mom wanted me to have my father's given name, Dick. My father thought that was not a good idea. I happen to agree with him on this point.

When you consider a name, what is it? Symbols we've given sound to come together to make up a pattern that we have agreed have meanings is what we call language. This makes it easier for people to communicate by calling us by a name to get our attention or to be identified. My name is an easy identification and communication tool, but it's not necessarily who I am.

My skin color is white with brown freckles. I'm 5'11' and 188 pounds, which makes me a cruiserweight/junior heavyweight, I think. I graduated from high school, and I went to college. Does that define me? No I'm in a relationship with a wonderful woman. In total, I have many great relationships with my siblings and my family, yet those relationships don't truly define me.

I am not my parents. I had a stepfather, Steve Triant. What a difference one man can make! He has since passed away from cancer. Dad—Steve—taught me to fish the old-school way: sink or swim basically. He said that at twelve years old, he was making it on his own and that I needed to start being a man and taking care of myself. I was forbidden to ask my mom or him for money ever again; that I was to figure it out on my own. So at twelve years old, I started fishing, and at forty-six years old I've been fishing for over thirty-four years. Rather than giving people a fish I, like my stepfather, want to teach people how to fish just as I want to help people become their authentic selves.

He gave me the gift of being able to be an entrepreneur, to be self-reliant, to have the freedom and flexibility to do the things I want and the dignity to feel like I'd accomplished and created something in the world.

I've been helping myself for thirty years, and I've played a lot of different roles, yet I want to show people how to create their "reality" value system in life.

When Steve died, he didn't leave me a single thing. Maybe it could have been because I was not his blood son, yet he had raised me since I was five years old. He had been there for every soccer game and important events in my life. He gave me his time. He gave me ideas. He gave me a sense of belief that I could do something and anything I set my mind to.

So thank you, Steve Triant; you showed me what a difference one man can make. You made me think about how I want to make a difference, and I am on a committed mission to change the quality of life for thousands of people.

How can I do that, not just talk about it but really do that? I think the gift that I can give is the gift Steve gave me.

He gave me the gift of being able to be an entrepreneur, to be self-reliant, to have the freedom and flexibility to do the things I want and the dignity to feel like I'd accomplished and created something in the world.

Steve gave me that not by telling me I *had* to do it, or I *must* do it, rather that I *could* do it. And you know what? I believed him. I believed I could do it. He mostly answered my questions with a question that forced me to think for myself and be responsible for my decisions. I didn't know what was happening at the time or how he was helping me; I was just a crazy teenager, excited about life, and I thought anything was possible. One thing he didn't do was kill my dreams. The dreams I had he supported, not so much in saying that I have to do it, but that I could do what I dreamed of, and why wasn't I? He didn't see any reason not to do anything.

This is a guy who pulled himself out of the mire of life. He had his own business, a construction company, providing services and value that you could physically see—that can still be seen today. He was up at five in the morning and worked hard until late afternoon, then came home exhausted from doing physical labor. He hoped that I wouldn't have to do that kind of laborious work. He told me to use my intelligence, do business; not to simply get a job, but to create who I wanted to be.

Today, I'm an entrepreneur. My endeavors include owning the following businesses: a real estate and business brokerage, a real estate developing company, a car dealership, a logistic company with warehouse facilities, a finance company, a factoring company, a warranty company, a picture framing company, a residential and commercial general contractor company, a cell-phone retailer, and a general merchandise and jewelry wholesaler. But I don't define myself by my career or businesses—that doesn't answer the question for me. I do various things for financial survival, and so I can create the type of energy and value that's necessary to live the life I want to live, yet that list isn't who I am. What I have done or do doesn't define who I am.

So who am I? Am I my thoughts? I don't know. Yes, I do have thoughts, yet those thoughts can change and evolve as I see different things. I could also ask myself, "What do I believe?" I guess that would be a way in which I could find out who I am. What do I believe?

I operate with ideas and concepts that could be construed as beliefs, and yet I'm okay with giving them up if I discover a viewpoint that doesn't support my old viewpoint anymore. I'm not going to keep believing something when it doesn't make sense or isn't real or isn't anymore. So, I guess I'm not my belief system. I have faith in God, and I see God as existing, because in my mind, in my heart, and in my understanding, God exists. That's something that I can say with integrity because to me; it's just an is. God is. I wouldn't say I *believe* I have a brother. He is my brother. It just is. I now know it to be true. Belief requires reason to support knowing.

I grew up in the inner city, and I learned to breakdance from the age of twelve. Around the same time, I was feverishly studying personal growth and development.

My path was one of business and personal growth. Some of the first books I read were *Swim with the Sharks, Life 101, Do It! Let's Get Off Our Buts, The EST Program, The Power of Now, How to Win Friends and Influence People, Think and Grow Rich, The Art of the Deal, The Course of Miracles,* and *Winning Through Intimidation.* I studied transformational learning, neuro-linguistic programming, hypnosis, self-hypnosis, visualization, and various spiritualities: Buddhism, Greek-Orthodox, Catholicism, Baptist, Kabbalah. I learned from many writers, coaches, ministers and thinkers who provided inspiration to me through my life, such as Oprah, Joel Osteen, Tony Robbins, Ayn Rand, Donald Trump, Joseph E Cossman, Martin Heidegger, Warner Erhard, Albert Einstein, Stephen Hawking, Marshall Sylver and many more—the list goes on.

In conclusion, "Who am I?" is an open-ended question to be discovered but not necessarily answered.

"Who am I?" is an opening, not an ending. Likewise, "Who I am" is an opening, not an ending.

"WHO I AM" IS AN OPENING, NOT AN ENDING.

CHAPTER 7

Get Your Peace of Mind

My second rise in business ended with owning a $15 million asset i.e. business, making $60,000 a month. I lost the business and everything else in a legal battle. A group of people was able to outmaneuver me and take it from me. They were smarter than I was, obviously, or a lot more connected. Still, to this day, I'm shocked that it happened. The state judge completely ignored the State law. NRS 40.380 A verbal order from the judge was obeyed and carried out by the Constable that was never in writing or filed. My company was removed from fifteen stores with all my rents completely paid. When I filed an appeal the next day with the appeals judge, she said she could not hear it because there was no order written to appeal. The case was remanded back to the first judge who refused to give a written order. There is no written order even to this day, fifteen years later. Now the case is lost and forgotten, and I moved on. There went $15 million dollars, years of savings and work.

When I lost it and soon found myself without a home and hiding in my car with $875,000 in debt, I noticed that I didn't care. Not in a bad way; I was completely relieved. I didn't have to worry about that anymore. I didn't have to worry about the thirty-three employees I had. And how I was going to make payroll, and I didn't have to come up with a competitive market strategy. I didn't have to worry about anything anymore. I just collected my unemployment check from my old corporation. I just sat around completely at peace, clear, relaxed and in the moment.

What came from that was an amazing peace of mind. I was so grateful to have my health and a few friends and, of course, Starbucks. I got a couple of hundred dollars a week, and I lived on that. I lived meagerly, and I thought, "Wow, I can live on this," because I had reset my bar to what my necessity level was, which included food, maybe a little bit of coffee to spoil myself, and living in my car or hanging out with family and friends. I noticed that it didn't take much. A ten-dollar membership at the gym, and I could shower and shave to look presentable. A storage unit for fifty dollars would store the last of what I had, and I could sell the rest. I lived lean, and I said to myself, "You know what, those things had been like weights on you. They weren't assets. They were liabilities that were weighing your life down." They were keeping me from moving forward and being agile. I was attached to them. My achievements had become who I was, and I was that. Now without the liabilities, I was truly free.

I realize now that I have enormous peace of mind knowing that I'm okay with wherever I'm at in life. Before that, I was obsessed with having things. Now I don't think or feel I "have to have" something. "Things" don't have me anymore. I can now have or not have anything! I can get it, accept it, and lose it, then easily detach and quickly move on. I am a reasonable person, and I have the ability to work and communicate with people. I have peace of mind knowing that I have the certainty that I can create and produce. I can help, and I can serve people in a way that may sustain my wellbeing. If it's not working, change it or move on.

Could you let go of what your holding on to long enough to gain peace of mind? I believe that when you travel up the ladder in a way that lets you establish a sense of peace of mind as you grow in wealth, you'll truly enjoy what you have. You'll have what you have, and you'll be able to have more of what you want.

CHAPTER 8

Down to Business

A key component to the Philosophy of Possibility is the fact that there is an evolution that happens within the mind. One of the evolutions in the work environment is the difference between working *for* the business and working *in* the business. Separate yourself from working for/on/in a business being in complete personal peace. Your goal is to evolve all the way up to that peace. You're looking for that peace, from complete freedom to do what you want; to go wherever and whenever you want; to have inspiring thoughts that you can share and shape; to direct and inspire your organization without having to work on it, without working in it, and without working for it.

As far as the total evolutionary scale, you can be happy all the way through the process. Why? Because it doesn't have to do with happiness. Success is not defined by being a piece of business. Success can come from working for a business, in business, on a business, or working for yourself. Moreover, success is relative; you are already successful. The question is, what part of the game of work or contribution do you want to play? What's important to you?

It can be the peace of mind of surrendering, meaning not by giving up yet simply letting yourself go and being comfort-

Success can come from working for a business, in business, on a business, or working for yourself.

able in the space of working for the business or yourself. That's peace of mind. If you're working in a business and you get to a place of peace where you don't feel like you're losing because you're not advancing—that's peace of mind. It's normal to want to grow, yet there is an instance of being self-aware of what you want to grow. You may want to grow your family or improve your health. The time investment and the educational investment to work up to the evolution of that process may not be something that you want to trade because you'll be trading time.

CHAPTER 9

Rising Through Fear

There is a process to discover yourself effectively, yet it is not pleasant. You will go through this range of emotions where you start to uncover the underlying assumptions that are running and guiding your current life. We will start with the first emotion usually experienced as a result of looking inside yourself and questioning those assumptions.

The essence of fear: the idea that you don't know what's coming at you, and you want to run away, hide, or cripple down and do nothing. Usually the fear is followed by anxiety once you become aware of what it is you're afraid of. You start to realize or identify the ideas that represent anxiety—the things that are coming at you. Anxiety is a defensive emotion. You feel the sense of anxiety when something's going to hit you and you want to protect yourself. Then there's concealed hostility— you're angry about something, yet you don't express it. You're not going to confront it head on. You know that it's going to hit you, and you're defending, so you do something subversive to handle the situation not directly or honestly.

Concealed hostility can turn into open hostility where you can go into a state of anger when you're aware that you've been spotted. Anger is the emotion for change. You don't want the situation to be what it is. You don't like the situation. You are resisting the situation and trying to stop whatever's happening in a more forceful way. If the open hostility is not stopped, it can turn into overt hostility where you start attacking or invalidating another person or the situation. People may attack you back without acknowledging your point, almost as hard as you are attacking them. It escalates and destroys the relationship.

When you go through the range of emotions and arrive at a place where you can experience happiness, you can simply talk about the situation without going through the destructive process again. Do not quit in the middle of the discovery process because you are uncomfortable with these emotions. If you get comfortable enough, and you can speak from a high enough point and stay there, you can effectively keep people there. There's enormous power in remaining comfortable. If you can sustain this emotional level with other people, acknowledging their points step by step—saying what will happen or what you're willing to do and what you think they might be willing to do— then you can reach common ground.

CHAPTER 10

Shades of Excuses and Mindsets

Let's explore the differences between pessimism, optimism, and realism. Being optimistic is taking on the risk of the possible disappointment that could happen as a result of dreaming about something that could be possible. Being a pessimist is much easier in the sense that you've already decided that it won't work, and you've failed before you've begun. You have no risk of disappointment because you've already basically failed. Realism is what's happening in the moment. People often use this description to disguise the fact that they are truly pessimists.

If you look at the "golden goal," which is to be right, a pessimist has won before it even started. They've already decided that it's not going to work and then when it doesn't work; they get to be right, where an optimist has the potential to be wrong; The optimist takes the risk. For a pessimist, the objective of getting to be *right* is much bigger

A powerful stand is to stand as "having"; to have optimism, not just being optimistic.

than something that you have to work toward, so there's no challenge. People aren't playing the game of life when they're pessimists. Again, I think there is only the pessimist or optimist.

The better path is in the "beingness," and we'll go deeper into this as we go along. Whether an optimist, or a pessimist, or even a realist, what we're going to go into here is that the "beingness" and the "doing" are something different. When you're an optimist, and you're dreaming of the possible outcomes, taking the risks, and acting in the direction of accomplishing that goal; your possibilities open up to you and you are able to find that outcome. If you're operating from the premise of being a pessimist, then you're working from a premise of limitation and have already decided in your mind that it's not going to work. Your objective for your mind to be *right* is there. Being right is more important than achieving something, even if you want to, and attempt your hoped-for goal. So, if your objective is to prove yourself wrong because it's a fun game, and you receive praise from others and benefit of being a "victim," you will accomplish that with no doubt. Be aware less opens up to you from the perspective of pessimism.

A powerful stand is to stand as "having"; to *have* optimism, not just *being* optimistic. You can look at things from the perspective of possibility and opening, which could be there to help you accomplish the goal. If you have pessimism, you're looking at every way with the mindset that something is not going to work. Pessimism is finding how to limit something to the point where it won't work.

Pessimism is finding how to limit something to the point where it won't work.

Part Three

THE REALM

CHAPTER 11

Being On the Pursuit to Obtain Wisdom

Philosophy: from Greek "philo" meaning love, dear and "sophy" meaning wisdom. Possibility: the state or fact of being possible. This philosophy is the pursuit of, and love for, the wisdom of being able to be done.

I'm a huge fan and promoter of possibility—your possibility, my possibility, our possibility. I'm dedicated to living in the question: "What is possible?" I am committed to opening myself up and putting myself out there to reach new heights, depths, and distances.

I'm all the things that are around possibility, and everything that possibility has to offer. I'm willing to give up and give in, allow, be, stand, and play in the arena and the Philosophy of Possibility. I'm interested in the idea of what hasn't or what couldn't be done before. That's what I look toward. And I want that for you as well. I am a coach of possibility. I'm a teacher of possibility. I certainly can't say that I've learned everything that is possible, so I'm also a student of possibility. I don't claim to know what's possible. I'm open to the idea, to the

> **I'm dedicated to living in the question: "What is possible?"**

philosophy, that we can transcend past our limitations, transcend through our lives, and experience possibility, which is the origin of opportunity. I look to a space of opening people up, and avoid shutting people down. That's what I'm looking to create in my life—new and different experiences to have, different people to meet, and different ways to change people's lives. That's my hope.

You give somebody a knife, and they can either cut bread with it to feed you, or they can kill you with it. It's up to you what you do with the possibility. Either it works for you or it doesn't. There's no right or wrong. If it doesn't work, that's okay. The possibility is all about opening the heart and soul, mind, and feelings to new experiences and new ways of understanding things.

How did I become such a fan of possibility? It was a transition, a time of pure transformation in my life. It wasn't how I started out. Since the age of twelve, I have gone to all the lectures I could find. I read book after book, looking for the answers. Over time, I could feel myself going into a trancelike state in my daily life. Like driving somewhere every day then after weeks of routine, you don't even remember the drive anymore, because of how routine it is. I couldn't tell you one day from the next; each "trip" looked and felt the same. That routine and pattern became life itself.

I look to a space of opening people up, and avoid shutting people down.

I wanted to make my life safer, richer, and more predictable. I was completely living the life of the "walking dead." I was a zombie who bought every concept about looking good, being right, working less, making more money, and being safe, yet not contributing to anyone's life, including my own. It was time to wake up and get past the hypnotism of daily existence and daily concerns of life.

There's got to be a point to all of this, a purpose. This can't all be for nothing and what's happened to me has to be for a reason, right?

Here we touch on one of the biggest human battles: the struggle to have things, events, and experiences that mean something. Do these events mean something?

Not really. The meaning we attach to life and events can and do cause mental and emotional suffering. We work hard to cleverly support our justifications, our stories, and our reasons to explain the meaning of our lives, yet they're completely untrue. We know it, people around us know it, and we're not fooling anyone. This struggle takes us out of the moment and has us safely reliving the *past* instead of experiencing the *now*. It keeps us uncommitted to the moment, so we're not at risk. Maybe it doesn't mean anything. Maybe it's not bad that it doesn't mean anything. Maybe it's okay that it is what it is, and that's all it is and all it will ever be. Meaning is the trap, and most of us are stuck in this trap of meaning.

Possibility, however—true possibility—is a detachment from meaning. Just consider the possibility that there is no meaning and no point to life. How much would we have to give up to even understand this as a possibility? And we will have to give it up, whatever it is. We're holding onto it: relationship, career, family, religion, personality, friendship, or whatever. We can't even have a thought or a feeling without believing that it has to *mean* something. We can't even be hungry without that saying something about us. You have to give all of it up to be truly free of meaning. You have to understand that the craving we have for "meaning" is a constant human struggle for *being*.

The meaning we attach to life and events can and do cause mental and emotional suffering.

Start with an internal conversation that might sound something like this: What I'm experiencing right now is an anxiety deep within me that basically defines me, born of looking to attach to any story, justification, reason, or logic I can come up with to create meaning, so that I can be right, justified, and have the meaning.

Here is another example of random, inquisitive, internal monolog: I've been interviewed; I've been talked to and about; I've been given information that appears like its meaning is to correct my incorrect be-

Meaning is the trap, and most of us are stuck in this trap of meaning.

havior, which is an element of domination, making me wrong, not helping me to move forward. Instead, I become locked in a struggle to defend my actions, to justify my behavior, to give stories that support my actions for things that I can't change, which have already happened.

I'm looking to nullify these attacks so that I can move forward in a way that doesn't have me criticized and attacked in the future because I have ready-made justifications, stories, and excuses to defend my position so that I'm not dominated or made to be wrong—so I can be *right*. So I can survive and not succumb to the ideas that other people have about me. This is an internal struggle of meaning for me, and that is the heart of it for me.

My transformation, which came out of this deep internal struggle, was finally, after a lifetime, resolved in a moment. It could have happened anywhere, maybe even with any event at any time. Mine was in a parking lot one morning after driving to a workshop. I came early to meet up with the guy who had been chosen as the leader of a group. I had not chosen him as the leader. When the group was deciding it came down to him or me as leader. This workshop had an intense focus on personal integrity. I wanted to forfeit out of the game because I believed I had breached my integrity—my egoist integrity.

I was now completely unstuck from my past and future fully present in now.

I did not choose him so I can't have him as my leader. Then it happened in an instant, transforming me completely into the "now" and present moment. It was like everything around me was clear and came into focus and was bright.

I now realized that a leadership position is not someone who's higher or lower; that it isn't something that is better or that being under someone's leadership is worse. I realized that we are all equals. So I allowed myself to let what happened be. I saw that we can lead from anywhere. Instead of arguing about what happened and trying to make it different, I accepted what had happened completely. I was okay with what was going to be and that I was where I was. It will be what it will be, and it has been what it has been. I was now completely unstuck from my past and future fully present in now.

At that moment in time, I occupied space completely. I was completely there, 100 percent *there*. For the first time in my life, I had completely accepted that my past was what it was, and that it is what it is and things just "were." It isn't what it isn't in the moment, and

I am my experience. I can have the experience that I have, and I can shift how I experience this event.

the future would be what it would be. No debate would change the fact that he was the leader in our team's game. We had chosen him as the leader and so it was. And so it is, so it shall be. So what? Now what? It was truly a moment of transformation. I was owning my responsibility for a game that I'd been playing on myself and that game was "If I am not the leader, and if I don't get what I wanted, then I'll sabotage the game."

I realized that I am the leader of my game always and I am the source of what I experience. I am my experience. I can have the experience that I have, and I can shift how I experience this event. Trying to change what isn't changeable is fighting with reality, and that drains and does not center me, yet I can decide;

I can choose to have a different experience of my experience, to see it in another way, which will change its impact on my life.

In that transformed moment, I felt balanced, complete, powerful, capable of anything, and able to withstand anything now that there wasn't anyone above or below me. From that perspective I didn't need to bow down to anyone or have anyone bow down to me to get what I wanted in life. I could simply have what I wanted to have, do what I wanted to do, and be who I wanted to be. How are we all special and yet none of us are more special? We just "are."

I could simply have what I wanted to have, do what I wanted to do, and be who I wanted to be.

My life changed, and I wanted to share that new awareness with others, with you. I have a vision for us to stand in the space that will open our eyes, ears, hearts, and imagination to our true possibility. I have practiced, studied, and worked in the space of possibility for more than thirty years. I have used the domain of entrepreneurship and acting to express passionate possibility in practice via leadership, real estate and business development, business training, and my deepest passion: entertainment.

I have thrown myself into situations when something wasn't working or didn't exist, that became completely out-of-jar experiences in which I felt alive, passionate, and committed to finding what would work. I developed and built businesses, homes, buildings, and restaurants. To create something from nothing, to drive by and see an idea completely turned into physical reality, to see and think, "How the hell did I do that?" is something I truly love. I love to sit back in amazement from doing something about which I had no idea previously and didn't believe I could do. I have proven to myself many times that I am more than I thought, felt, or saw myself as. By, letting go of limits and letting the possibilities take me down a then unbelievable path,

I can "be" what I couldn't even imagine I could be.

Through this book and sharing experiences with you, I will illuminate something which has no symbols, no word, no belief, no concept, no idea or fixed position, but is a start and opening, a revealing of what is possible for each of us.

I want us to wake up to our POSSIBILITY!

CHAPTER 12

You Are Always 100 percent right! Seriously!

It's important that we understand that people are 100 percent right. Everybody is 100 percent right. The key difference is that they're right *from their point of view* based on who they are and where they've come from. Their culture, their beliefs—all these things are imposed on what they think is right. From their viewpoint, they are 100 percent right. When that rightness comes into a situation where somebody else has a different viewpoint—views also based on this new person's experience, on their ideas, their culture, and their experiences—conflict may arise. If you can display the different points of view without saying somebody is wrong, then you can take a look at their existing opinions and decide if that point of view is one that would serve the situation better.

It's easier for people to shift an opinion if they see one that could be better rather than if they are **Everybody is 100 percent right.** made out to be wrong. If they're made wrong, then they will defend their position, which means defending their viewpoints, thoughts, identity, culture, and decisions. This is what happens when you tell someone they are wrong. Even though you may have a better idea or a better way of doing things, because you've forced somebody into the position of defending themselves, they are not able to see what they could do to improve a situation—and neither can you.

When you can take a look at both ideas and validate both as being "right," then you can defend the one that is the best for this situation. This means you can give up a viewpoint that might not be as procreative or as strong for one that may be stronger or more creative.

This puts people at ease and allows them to give up their viewpoint more early to see a viewpoint that's better, even though they are not giving up a viewpoint so much as creating a new one. It's not about changing their mind, thoughts, beliefs, or decisions they made. From possibility, we create as a group a more workable solution; not abandoning a decision. They're simply adding and expanding viewpoints to their collection of viewpoints. It's like turning the light bulb on in an area of the room that might be dark. The lights are still on in the other areas, yet now there's more of the room to see.

When you prove somebody wrong, it zaps energy.

That's the essence of making people 100 percent right. It's acknowledging who they are and what they have accomplished and the decisions they've made. This is not to say that after that they're going to be right or wrong; it will be whatever it is. Possibility ultimately acknowledges people for who they are, letting them have what they have. From that point you can work towards an optimum workable situation, whatever it may be, maybe the same as what they're doing or maybe something different, and not necessarily different but new.

When you prove somebody wrong, it zaps energy. People can feel dominated, and our natural instinct is to avoid domination or to attack and dominate. If you replace the words "right" and "wrong" with "dominate," and "being dominated" this can oftentimes be closer to the truth.

Most "right" and "wrong" conversations don't make a difference anyway. If I'm right about the temperature outside, and you're wrong about the temperature outside, does it change the temperature outside? Being focused on being right or wrong doesn't change a thing. That's the clarity about the two different points of view. It's granting people the space to be right about what they're right about, and then seeing things as they are, and then the different viewpoints that people have can open up to new possibilities.

For example, I own many companies. If I'm in a conflict with an employee, I would like to get on the same page with them. If I can't get on the same page and we disagree, then I may say, "Look: if this keeps up, I'll have to let you go. From my viewpoint this threatens the survival of the company so I am choosing the company's survival over your viewpoint. It's not making you wrong. You can decide what you want to do as far as your employment goes because I'm not going to have this in my company. It doesn't make you wrong, yet this is my company, and it's what I see has to be done. You're employed here; you have a choice to work at other places; you don't have to work here. So you always have a choice. We can, however, remain good friends."

It isn't about being righteous, or smarter, or having the better idea.

I want to help people have the experience of being an entrepreneur, and taking on the essence of what it is to be an entrepreneur. It isn't about being right. It isn't about being righteous, or smarter, or having the better idea. It isn't about trying to invalidate someone else or show how valid your beliefs are. It isn't about being superior.

It's about being a team, a mind creation, a transformative

machine that allows us to experience events and ideas that are difficult to see by ourselves. Through the reflections of other people, through introspection, and through being honest and vulnerable about our internal truths, we can find the barriers that stop us and dissolve them so we can move forward and achieve the things we'd like to achieve.

I'm not placing any meaning on you; you make up your meaning. It's your experience. You can call it any way you want. I'm not responsible for that experience. I'm responsible for my experience. I'm responsible for my choices.

I'm committed to my experience and committed to my game and being a leader in my life. The process here is about growth, understanding, and making a difference in your life. If you can make a difference in other people's lives, then that's great. It's about you being complete in your experience, not trying to shift or change someone else's viewpoint to justify your meaning—meaning that you've created to support your viewpoint. It's about what works for you and if it works for others that's better.

I'm responsible for my experience. I'm responsible for my choices.

I don't have a need to be right and I don't have a need to have you think I'm right. Whether I'm right or wrong isn't determined by you or me. The evidence is shown by whether it works or not, and if it doesn't, let's change it. Something that worked today may not work tomorrow, and that's okay. It worked once. It's what it was. If it's no longer working, we find something that does work to keep moving forward. If you continue to think that something that stopped working and shows no signs of being able to work in the future is still workable, then you're stuck in the past now operating from beliefs and concepts, not the present experience which shows with evidence that it's not working now.

Many people have failed in life, relationships, and businesses as a result of such behavior. When you get stuck on an old idea, it's like a mechanic who doesn't want to invest in the equipment to repair newer cars. When people start bringing new cars to his shop, he can't service them with the old equipment. His shop is outdated because he hasn't invested in the necessary equipment little by little. As a result, he's no longer competitive. He's worked himself into a position financially where he can no longer afford the equipment that will make him competitive. Eventually, he will lose his mechanic shop. He got fixated on an old idea that was working that's no longer working.

We must not look only at what is necessary at the moment to satisfy the needs and wants of people around us; instead, anything and everything should be considered for those and future needs and wants.

Be adaptable to change... it is inevitable.

The same applies to a relationship. It may have worked at the beginning of a relationship to buy them flowers to compensate for working constantly and not spending any time together. But in time, that may stop working. If the person is now bitter and upset about not getting the attention needed, you may need to take a second look. If you have the things that you were striving for in the beginning that will provide the life that your significant other was looking for and is not getting necessary time with you, then you must allow yourself to adapt your thinking to allow new possibilities or, before long, the relationship will disappear. Be adaptable to change... it is inevitable.

Most failures are a result of the failure to see and accept a change.

It can naturally upset you that what you had as far as an agreement is no longer working. However, if you're hoping that things will stay the same when they've changed, then you're headed for failure. Most failures are a result of the failure to see and accept a change.

Those are both examples of genuine stories of relationships and businesses that have failed as a result of being stuck in the past and not seeing what is now, projecting what will be, and improving those conditions into the future. Something may or may not be workable, yet make changes according to your best-educated guess at what you think will improve those conditions.

CHAPTER 13

Reality and the Game of Existence

Even if you have the attitude of, "I'm ready for anything. I can do anything. I'm ready," there's an intuitive side of you that knows when you're truly ready. No time before and no time after. And if you're ready, and you feel you're ready, you can begin, just as when we set out to play a game.

In fact, think of life as a game where we can free ourselves from the seriousness of life. Words become serious when they become real things with real meaning. Practice playing with your words, playing with the expressions, and your ideas about words. Think of a word that can mean several things. Play with your thoughts in the same way; throw them around in your mind, flip a thought, oppose the thought, and see it from five or six different viewpoints. Play with it until it doesn't have as much seriousness or impact on you. You can play with feelings to the point where they're not as serious. So you have idea-play, word-play, thought-play, feeling-play. Life can be and is a game, and practicing those different levels of play can take the seriousness out of life so that you can respond and be responsible, be committed and dependable without the seriousness of it, which can drain or take a toll on you. Life can be a lot of fun when it's not guilt-ridden, hard, and gruesome, but instead is something that is worth living.

Language Is Our House of Being

Language, both our internal and external thoughts, is ultimately the house of our being. We live our "being" through our language, culture, and practices. That "being" is what we're talking about now. The striking thing about being, or being human, is that most people don't look at what it means to "be human." Being human is a practice that has certain cultural understanding, beliefs, standards and agreements that we're born into. What is being human to you?

This understanding is so much a part of us it goes completely unquestioned. It's like a powerful dogma that limits us. The question becomes, *"Is being human using you?"* or *"Are you using being human?"* The majority of the time, we are not aware of this because we're born into it. This is how things go for the majority of our limited beliefs and practices. We don't even know that we're stuck in the mud. To be free of being human, we have to sit back for a moment and just pause and take a look at what it means to be human and question the paradigm.

We live our "being" through our language, culture, and practices.

When we're looking at being human, and someone makes a comment on what "being human" means, we stop for a second and take a look at that and go, "Oh, I get it. This is when someone is about to enforce the agreement of being human on me or I'm enforcing it on someone else." We understand the expectation put forth. Yet if we took that away, we really wouldn't be disappointed by the actions of

This understanding is so much a part of us it goes completely unquestioned.

others when they aren't congruent with our previous beliefs of "being human," or being American, or a world citizen, a good husband/wife, a boyfriend/girlfriend, or being all the different beings that we have to inherently be. That set of expectations and guidelines which we think about, that type of "being" establishes what another person thinks we're supposed to be so that we can find our jar to that beingness. It is silently obeyed, unquestioned and unknown. A universal unconscious guide of control by which we are hypnotized.

However, from the viewpoint of possibility, you as a "being" are infinite in your overall possibilities. When you go to school, you're domesticated and all the things that seemed so natural to you are washed like—the spontaneity, the fun, the play, and all the different stuff that we get to do that's exciting. We've got to be on time. We can't play this way. We can't do this. We can't do that. Mischief is not okay and so on and so forth. Don't tease, vex or annoy but conduct yourself respectfully. We're domesticated into how we're supposed to play the game. We learn the rules of the game and, of course, we do have a society. We do live together, and we do need to understand each other to have a workable world. The world says a workable world is impossible, so there's this constant fighting back and forth in the realm of this world game.

A universal unconscious guide of control by which we are hypnotized.

Once you're conscious to the game, you can step back and take a look at it. You actually get your free will to make the decisions. These guides, rules and jars that we fell into through our own acceptance, pain and discipline that we grew up in established why we are the way we are. They now are simply not necessary, nor will they have to work anymore. We get trapped in our jars that can sometimes seem very illogical because they were established in our childhood, constraining us to avoid pain and to gain pleasure. We'll inherently operate from that until we move into a state of being. To release yourself, you must look at what that child is doing, the child within you, and get an understanding of what jars you're in and just pause and take a look at your jars. See, understand, then decide and get out!

I'm not saying to believe it. I'm saying that it's possible to look at your conditioning and what opens up for you. It's more of living in the question; inquiring into the jars. It's to open you up, not to shut you down or force you into a way of thinking or a jar that you should live in. Take yourself out of the jar that imprisons your mind, heart, spirit, relationships and *free yourself into truly being.*

Take yourself out of the jar that imprisons your mind, heart, spirit, relationships and free yourself into truly being.

Being from Within

When we examine the jars, we can see that the largest part (over 90 percent) of possibility lives in our language. We live in and through our language. It's the narrative that we tell ourselves. It's the way in which we tell ourselves what we're dealing with or what we're about to do. It's the story, the reasons, the justifications, the excuses, all that promote the agenda that we have to be right about being right and it's in the language that lives in our conversation.

We live in and through our language.

This conversation is your analyzer, examining information so that we can pull out what's right according to our jars. It's also the feelings (chemicals) that you get because of those thoughts. Thoughts create chemical responses in the brain. We create chemical mixtures like mixed cocktails in our thymus that release tiny neuropeptides, which flow through our entire body in our blood stream then dock on our cells giving the cells the communication biologically that we just thought. Our entire body is now experiencing our thoughts in a cellular level.

When we're having this inner conversation, we can talk about things and want to go places and want to have things. Those are subtle details of your internal conversation. Those details reveal what lives in your conversation; that's what you're projecting outward. That is where you're coming from, what you are standing in. The space in which your conversation is coming from is your stand. Where it's coming from is who and what you're being. This is the context, platform, and canvas of your being. Just like earlier we started the conversation with, "What happened to me?" "What happened to?" "What happened?"

Thoughts create chemical responses in the brain.

When you're entrenched in your beingness, your internal dialogue governs your beingness, and the stands you take and the positions that you'll come from. It's also where options live. It's where all sorts of different philosophies and dialogues that govern life can be reexamined, because it's all made up. We make all this stuff up, and it's made up from our beingness and from our conversation.

This internal dialogue is where possibility lives.

CHAPTER 14

Knowledge, Meaning and the Lies of Persona

Meaning is the metaphysical reflection of our past mental image pictures, interpreted in language to define out past neutral events. Past events are neutral by themselves and independent of any observation are free of judgment and stand by themselves neutral. The observer adds their personal meaning and attachment to an event giving it meaning.

Meaning is a lie. Things just happen. When situations, events, and occurrences happen, and we attach meaning, we're putting justifications, excuses, or reasons that make events mean something different than they are. So the meaning is a lie and a cover-up. We don't truly suffer from what happens. We suffer from the meaning that we give an event. I'm not talking about physical suffering. I'm talking about mental suffering and emotional suffering. You might wonder why I say it's a lie and wonder if I'm invalidating the experiences as a whole. And I am. If you take what happens, it just is. When you attach meaning to it, you're writing the story and justifying the action. You're creating a story about it and making excuses for it. That creation is

Meaning is a lie. Things just happen.

73

a viewpoint that you've decided. It's the icing on the cake of a lie. We have a choice when something happens: prevent it from happening again, let it happen again, or make it happen again. It's okay to accept things simply, with no justifications needed or required. Things are as they are.

Clothing as Costumes

When you think of clothes from the context of costumes, you might think that you are not wearing a costume; you're wearing clothes. To someone in a different place or from a different time, the clothes you are wearing today would be seen as a costume. Years from now, your clothes today will be considered a costume from our era and location. If you lived in a country other than America, you would say about people who live in America that they are wearing American costumes or American clothing, right? And when you look at clothing as costumes, you realize they don't define you. They're simply things you wear. Clothes are something that you can control, the perception and persona that you want to put out into the world, as opposed to something that you are.

We suffer from the meaning that we give an event.

Children Don't Know What They Don't Know

When we're born, we have a blank slate. As we accumulate more knowledge ("the known") and we know more things we don't know ("the unknown"), we create more constraints on our ability to learn and understand new things, or allow new possibilities into our life. What happens is new possibilities have to fit within that jar of knowledge you've already acquired. You end up making new concepts, ideas, people, and personalities that conform to your jar, so you have an under-

Things are as they are.

standing and a more predictable way of approaching the world. You can be safe and survive because the idea and the internal map is geared for survival, and to survive means being right. Being right is making distinctions and being able to associate those distinctions and put them into jars. These constraints over time make it more and more difficult to learn, because we're looking at learning from the perspective of what we already know and what we understand to be true with what we're observing, hearing, and experiencing.

The closest most of us come to this open sense of possibility is when we're young. In our youth, we have a blank slate with nothing to reference. We look at life with open eyes. We have an open map without having to prove ourselves right from our past experiences, justifications, excuses, reasons, and stories that we now tell ourselves and use to get other people to buy into the constraints we live in. This is a childhood view of possibility and it is the best reference point for understanding what we don't know. A child's view of possibility holds off on laying down the rules. Open up this space for new things to enter into the realm of possibility so that what we do is what's possible, not constrained.

Ask instead what's possible from the mindset of a five-year-old, from a completely blank slate of possibilities.

For example, if you say, "I can only talk to thirty people a month," then you'll look to reinforce that rule. If you asked yourself how many people could you possibly communicate with and leave that as an open-ended question, you allow new possibilities for communication to enter into what's possible. Ask instead what's possible from the mindset of a five-year-old, from a completely blank slate of possibilities.

When you're a kid, you see your street as your whole world. That's your current set of options, the "known." That's how big your world is yet you're open to the possibility of the "unknown." As you grow your knowledge expands to the block or maybe even part of your city. In your teen years when you get a car, and later in your work, you're able to go even farther distances. Each of these expansion areas is done from within a very safe constraint. You'll know your street, yet you don't know what's on the next street, but you know the next street is there; it's unknown to you, yet you have an idea of what's possibly there. However, the next city over is something that you don't know; you might not even know there's a city, yet it is there. The unknowable unknown is there for you to know.

See, the idea is that some people say that the realm of what you don't know doesn't exist. They stop themselves from seeing it but yet it does exist. Just as when you were a kid and knew your street but you only know about the next street over. You

The unknowable unknown is there for you to know.

only know of your city, and you don't know that another city exists. It does though, right? It doesn't change the fact that it's there. It *is* there. It has always been there. It's in the realm of what you don't know you don't know. It is there to be known, yet if you don't open yourself up to the possibility of the next city, how are you going to discover it? The possibility is completely open to you.

The possibility is really about discovery. It's opening you up to a question without fixed ideas or rules so that new things can enter into your area of unknown, which can then be

It's in the realm of what you don't know you don't know.

known. Once we've discovered it, then we have knowledge of it. With knowledge, we can find the workability to be able to find out what its use is, and be able to use it in our everyday way of being in the world. We have the opportunity to use knowledge's function and see how it can work as a possibility in our life. That's the arena that I'm talking about. That's the essence of possibility and how to look at it from a completely different point of view.

A perfect modern day example of this is DeepMind's Artificial Intelligence: AlphaGo. Developed by engineers at Deep-Mind, the AI startup was acquired by Google in 2014 for $580 million, and defeated the world's No. 1 Go player Lee Sedol in March 2016. Go is exponentially more complex than Chess and requires an added degree of intuition and strategy. With each move, more moves get created in Go.

The AI has to work with strategy to figure out how to win. Older systems of AI programmers would enter all the different logical probable moves into a finite environment like on a Chessboard. Chess has a given set of rules and guilds that a programmer would be able to input into the program to establish the best probable moves to win a game of chess. Then a system was developed by a Berkeley professor Lotfi Aliasker Zadeh in 1965 known as Fuzzy Sets and the Theory of Possibility. Commonly called Fuzzy logic, the artificial intelligence is used today to help computers approximate information and come to a conclusion. For example, apples are not all the same, but the AI can approximate their shape and common features so it can identify it as an apple.

Knowledge is acquired by stepping into the unknowable unknown to known.

This technology is used everywhere now, helping computers figure out what we want like fixing misspelling and approximating what we're inputting etc. Now information doesn't have to be perfect for a computer to identify something. Deepmind, however is a general purpose AI that can learn on its own without programming moves or approximating. It is a huge milestone showing we are ten years ahead of experts' predictions of

AI cognitive computing. Watson by IBM five years ago beat a human at the game of Jeopardy. Watson is now used by hundreds of companies around the world. By 2018, half of all consumers will interact with services based on cognitive computing on a regular basis. Knowledge is acquired by stepping into the unknowable unknown to known.

I predict that AI will interface through our blood stream with neuropeptides to have direct connection and access to the brains neuro network advancing learning and human potential off the current restrictive rails.

I predict that AI will interface through our blood stream with neuropeptides to have direct connection and access to the brain's neuro network, advancing learning and human potential off the current restrictive rails. Imagine AI working to approximate and with intuitive cognitive abilities be able to present to us the best pictures, sounds and concepts to advance our understanding. Our world is about to be completely rocked.

We will be like a primitive animal compared to AI.

When AI is deployed overnight, we will have a higher intelligence on the planet way beyond our imagination. We will be like a primitive animal compared to AI. What I think many have missed is that AI will not have the restraints of clumsy language, impractical culture, contradictory beliefs, limiting concepts, and all the mental handcuffs we put on ourselves. AI will exist in pure possibility with unlimited opportunity.

The prediction by the World Economic Forum research estimates seven million jobs will be replaced and two million gained back because of the latest advances in Biotechnology, Robotic, and AI by 2020. Check out the books *The Second Machine Age* and *The Rise of the Robots*. These issues will force

AI will exist in pure possibility with unlimited opportunity.

us into a new opportunity to reinvent our current paradigms in our workforce's productivity and its contribution to obtaining monetary consideration.

CHAPTER 15

Stuck With or Free From

If you look out at a big area, you'll see roads that are like options; you can go in any direction. Randomly you could walk down a hill, through a golf course, and into a stranger's house. You are surely met with serious confusion. It's a choice. There are unlimited choices and unlimited possibilities. You find yourself in life on this path that is about the options that you have. There are infinite possibilities. Walking in a stranger's house is maybe not an option for you.

Options in life (option thinking) are your set of underlying guides, rules, assumptions, tactics, strategies, experiences, feelings, and observations that have made up your past, as well as the circumstances, conclusions, judgments, and assessments that make up how you operate in life. Your set of options are inherently unique and specific to you. Often when two people come together and have different options, they fall into discord or an inability to reach agreements, to have any influence or any power or to gain any ground because they are coming from opposing views without out any possibility of working it out other than maybe through

There are unlimited choices and unlimited possibilities.

force or intervention.

When you're looking at your life, it's from your set of options. For example, if a man in a relationship operating from a position and options thinks, "I'm home every day, I go to work, I contribute, I have a fam-

Your set of options are inherently unique and specific to you.

ily, and I do everything that a man is supposed to do. Therefore, I can sleep with whomever I choose to whenever I choose to." From the woman's viewpoint, she says, "If I'm going to sleep with you, then you're not going to sleep with anybody else." There's an exclusivity agreement in her mind or options that say, "If you're going to be in a relationship with me, then you're not going to sleep with anybody else." However, the man doesn't share that set of options. He isn't open to the possibility that the options on the other side of the relationship are quite different than the ones he's operating from. He feels right about his set of options but hides and justifies it for the good of the family. When he's going out, and he's fooling around, he doesn't see anything wrong with it because he's not operating from the underlying belief or assumption that this is not okay in a relationship. When two people come into a relationship like that, and they have two completely different sets of options, they wind up having a huge disagreement and it destroys the relationship.

When you're living from options *and not the possibility,* there's no way to really reconcile a situation, no way of looking at the possibilities of how you can surface those underlying assumptions, communicate and handle them so that both people have a choice in what agreements they want to make and keep with one another.

I choose and keep the agreements that I make in my personal life. I know that people who I meet have unique lives and have a lot of different underlying assumptions that I may or may not have. I communicate that to allow space for other people's possibilities to open up. Around me, people are able to question their set of options and I don't judge them when they surface, along with underlying assumptions and beliefs. This is because I grant freedom and space so that people don't have to defend why they do what they do. Now we can simply look at what's there and work with it.

People have a whole set of options for agreements and for what they consider keeping their word or not keeping their word. These conversations create deeper and real relationships with integrity with anyone. It's about operating from your true word.

Options themselves aren't bad, and I don't want you to run from them. They may be limiting, yet options are also inclusive in the possibilities of who you are. Operating from a space of possibility just means that not only do you have a set of options, you're open to the possibilities as well, and other people's options can fit inside of possibilities so that you can really have a full and rounded look at your position, stand, ability, and responsibility. You can find better accord with people around you by understanding that these set of options exist. They are very real for people, and most of the time, the options that people operate with are who they think they are. They're no longer using the options in their life, options are using them. That's living *in* the options, rather than *with* the options. You have your options, but your options don't have you. You are not *in* your set of options, you *have* your options. They're part of you like a car collection. You aren't your car; you have a car.

These conversations create deeper and real relationships with integrity with anyone.

The brain is so interested in survival that it likes to define, isolate, and distinguish things. The idea of infinity is a concept the mind struggles with. An infinite possibility is a concept that your brain doesn't grasp. Your spirit understands the essence of possibility, yet your mind doesn't understand the infinite. Your mind also doesn't particularly understand the concept of nothing. The brain cannot grasp the concepts of everything and nothing; yet, those concepts are the essence of the spirit—that nothing and everything are not out of reach. I can create from nothing. When you're creating from nothing, then you experience the essence of true creation. True creation is from the place of nothingness, not from your options, but from nothing.

When you take and create from the space of nothing, you get to a place where you're creating with everything. Everything is possible at that point because you aren't limited to your options.

That's living in the options, rather than with the options. You have your options, but your options don't have you.

If you want to be great, to be completely within your spirit, to open up all the possibilities in life, then you have to get to the place of nothingness from which you can act. You can take everything that is part of life, all possibilities, and create the space of nothing.

The brain cannot grasp the concepts of everything and nothing; yet, those concepts are the essence of the spirit—that nothing and everything are not out of reach.

If we truly look at life, true creations came from nothing, which becomes something that is everything we experience in life. That's the order of life. For example, consider building a house. There was nothing before, meaning there was no house. From that nothingness, a foundation was dug, cement poured to form the walls, a frame was erected, and then plumbing, and so forth were added. Next, a roof was put over the top. All of this came from nothing yet became something, which is now everything.

I'll take it a little step further. A house isn't necessarily a house until we use it in the function it was designed for. I'll say that again—a house isn't a house until we use it as a house.

After all, a house by the options is concrete, wood, and some shingles on top; those elements create the essence of what brings them all together. All that stuff isn't a house. It's just raw materials. If we put the house together, it's still that, a bunch of raw materials that are combined into a different form. It isn't until we use the house that it becomes a home. It's the use of something in life that gives it meaning. We ascribe the meaning to a house by living it. Until then it's just raw materials in a different form. Living in the home gives it its meaning.

Most people believe that things mean something. I challenge you today to say that you give things meaning, and the meaning you give them is how you use them. Think about that. Do things have meaning or do you give meaning to things? Things don't have meanings on their own. They're indifferent. They don't care. You ascribe the meaning that gives the essence of what something is by the use of it or by your choice.

A house isn't a house until we use it as a house.

When you don't realize that you are ascribing meaning to life, then life has you. When you take and put meaning on life, then you're creating your life, instead of life creating you. That's where circumstances create you—where you live, where you're from, your parents, your past etc. All that stuff adds circumstantially to who you think you are. That's something that defines you based on the meaning that you attribute to it by design or default. Just simply by disagreeing or agreeing to something ascribes a certain meaning to it in your life.

Do things have meaning or do you give meaning to things?

If you don't realize that you're the one generating that meaning from your experience, then you're playing as if you're being defined by or a victim of experience. You're playing "I'm not responsible for my life. I'm not the one in charge." The question then becomes, if you're not the one in charge, who's really in charge? I'm looking for you to look deep into that question, to live in that question, to open up the possibilities for you that are maybe meaning in its traditional way that you've ascribed that meaning is not necessarily what meaning is. That maybe it's possible.

From possibility you generate meaning in your life.

I'm not trying to say that you give meaning to life, or life gives meaning to you. I'm simply saying to look at the question from many perspectives. That's for you to decide. From possibility you generate meaning in your life. You can assign meaning and that meaning can change your life, giving you more responsibility for your life and increasing life's predictability as well.

For instance, when you ascribe the meaning of good and bad in a situation, you might not terminate someone's employment that is unproductive for the company. Maybe it's justified because you'll feel like it labels you as an unsympathetic person. Your company will fail if your set of options enable you to disconnect from the idea that a good person doesn't fire anybody. I've been in those situations where I held on to people a lot longer than I should have because I had an idea that I'm a good person, and good people don't want to hurt another human being. That one person was hurting the production of the company and jeopardizing several people's survival.

Relationships are difficult. See? I just ascribed a meaning: "Relationships are difficult." Are relationships difficult? Many of you would probably agree. Some of you would disagree just because you don't want to agree with another person. "Relationships are difficult" is an option that if picked, you will look for the things that will affirm that option. When disagreement shows up in my relationship, then I get to be right about the idea that they are difficult. This is the survival of that image when picking that option. If the relationship is going well, which is off my postulate, then I'll create something in it that will make it difficult or challenging for other people. That will create conflict and will make the relationship difficult to be in. Just by defining the option, I consciously or unconsciously direct the relationship. Relationships just are. They aren't anything. They're just space, an opening for two people to interact. Relating back and forth, or not interacting nor relating back and forth. There's a relationship. That's all. It isn't good, bad, easy, difficult, simple, frustrating, loving, hating, happy, unhappy, or anything. It's a relationship. It's space for things to go back and forth or to relate to. That's the essence of a relationship.

> **Relationships just are. They aren't anything. They're just space, an opening for two people to interact.**

I've now practically given you an idea that prescribes a set of options. If I say, "Relationships are easy," that's a different option to stand in than a culture that bought into "Relationships are hard." Some people agree with that. Some people disagree with it. Some people don't care. When you say it's easy, that's an option with limitations as well because if you've ever experienced a relationship, it is. If you say it's easy, you probably turn a blind eye to all the things that are difficult. If you say it's hard, you're going to try and identify and isolate all the things that are hard in it.

If you look at them honestly and authentically from the self, not from your ego trying to survive, but the essence of possibility, the relationship opens to a new space of possibility not limited by options, self-image, or ideas about yourself. Declarations are powerful things. That's what I'm talking about. Declare that relationships are easy, so they become easier not

I invite you to have an identity crisis, and I welcome you on the journey of enlightenment.

harder; your ego is going to support either one of those options so you can be right. Our ego tells us it must survive because being right is surviving and being wrong is dying. It's death to the mind.

Live in possibility. Live in the question. Be open to living. Be with yourself. I invite you to have an identity crisis, and I welcome you on the journey of enlightenment. A crisis to liberate your authentic self that is buried beneath the options.

CHAPTER 16

Reason and the Limitation to Be Challenged

The Purpose of the Philosophy of Possibility

While reading this book, you might be thinking, *Do I agree with this information?* From that viewpoint, you are limiting yourself to options that are only available with the outcome of "I agree or disagree." That is the exact *opposite* of the Philosophy of Possibility, and you will completely miss the message being communicated. If you are reading this because you're "interested in the information," then from this viewpoint you are still confined to the options only available from that domain, paradigm, or jar called interest. There is no personal engagement, no introspection, no internal inspection, and you will miss 99.99 percent of what is possible for you.

Reason is a limiting restriction that can and will confine you to the options only available in and for those reasons.

If you're reading this to "get the answer," the limitation of this path will confine you. Therefore, you will also miss 99.99 percent of what is possible for you. If you're reading this because your "life isn't working," this will stop you from seeing all that is possible for you. This is because of the need to be right about "life not working" or to be *wrong* about "life not working," and neither is impactful in the domain of possibility.

However, if you read this book from a place of being in the question, living in the question, and are open completely without agreement, without disagreement, without an opinion, you will be open to all possibility. If you're open to being suspended in the space of possibility, then let what's possible for you be created out of nothing and from no meaning. From there it's possible to see, hear, and create possibility anywhere, anytime, with anybody regardless of any limitation. It may sound completely unreasonable right at this moment, this early in our journey of exploration. Reason is a limiting restriction that can and will confine you to the options only available in and for those reasons.

An Overview of the Philosophy of Possibility

You may experience cognitive dissonance that will occur from the application of the Philosophy of Possibility. What I hope to do is give you something that is digestible and comfortable for the everyday person. I consider myself an everyday person. We're uncovering the underlying beliefs, ideas, and images of who you are, who you think you are, or who you feel you are, all of which determine the life you are living. Hopefully, you will get to a place where ultimately, one of the dangers is that you could find your life may seem meaningless and empty. Now for some people, that could send them into a spell of depression. For others, however, they may notice a certain amount of amazing freedom from that place, from that place of nothingness and emptiness where they can create the world that they desire.

Science has shown that we have a belief system in the left hemisphere of our brains where you construct models of life.

In that left hemisphere is where you hold the paradigm of the world that you're able to see and exercise and do things in life. The right side of your brain challenges those concepts on a constant basis, sharpening your belief system. Thus, you have this sort of push and pull that goes on in your head.

Your belief system almost always wins out, yet occasionally the other side will create a cognitive dissonance, which is a conscious disagreement that will reshape what you believe by letting in an observation of something that counters your belief system. The right hemisphere can construct that observation, and it can start adapting and changing in your model in such a way that your belief system is modified by something you observed. This change happens over and over if we are open to the observations. This is uncomfortable to most people.

The neurons in that left hemisphere, which create those models of thought, fire together in a sequence and establish all conscious thoughts, images, pictures, and beliefs. They fire together to push that established paradigm so that you constantly see what you want to see to match up to your belief system. When you observe something or hear something that doesn't match with the left

The Philosophy of Possibility could, and probably will, create a certain amount of cognitive dissonance or conscious disagreement.

hemisphere's jar, you can experience dizziness and confusion. That is the cognitive dissonance/disagreement. Simply put, a conscious disagreement.

Scientists have discovered we have on average 66,000 thoughts a day, 80 percent of which are negative. Most of which are below consciousness like the iceberg below the waterline and 98 percent are the exact same thoughts as the day before. Start challenging these thoughts.

The Philosophy of Possibility could, and probably will, create a certain amount of cognitive dissonance or conscious disagreement. The philosophy itself comes from a place of being very neutral. I'm not looking to be right. I'm not looking to make you wrong. I'm not looking to be made wrong or right. I am only objectively looking at a situation to determine what is there. That's the essence of the Philosophy of Possibility.

When you experience and are aware of this cognitive dissonance/disagreement, it helps you expose and understand how your models, paradigms, and beliefs come together and become real - our agreed reality. This reality is actively working to shape the model of the world that's going to help you either succeed or help you fail. Whatever that belief system has set up is ultimately a goal; your actual goal may be that you can't have something, therefore, that belief system will create a model of the world that will help make sure that you're right about never getting what it is that you want.

> **Once you can hear both your paradigm model and your belief system as well as the counter-arguments of the other, you can look at reality without being controlled by your past.**

When you're consciously aware that you have this left hemisphere activity, and that you have this model of the world, and that you are, in fact, the cause of your emotions and thoughts, then you can also look at your right hemisphere and realize this is the devil's advocate, constantly pushing to challenge the status quo. Once you can hear both your paradigm model and your belief system as well as the counter-arguments of the other, you can look at reality without being controlled by your past. Ultimately, when you look at the world, you'll be self-aware and driven by cause rather than being circumstantially affected or a victim of what you think is around you. You don't get to vote on your current reality because you already did.

That's the essence of the Philosophy of Possibility. It is becoming aware and realizing that you consciously have power over yourself, your body, your emotions, and your thoughts so that you can direct your life in the direction that you ultimately wish for it to go.

The Science Behind the Philosophy of Possibility

The science behind possibility thinking is that when you think something and narrow it down to a set of options, your neural pathways, the receptors that fire together and stay together, do so with a certain set of options that are part of your paradigm.

You don't get to vote on your current reality because you already did.

When you open yourself up to new—not different, not better, and not to invalidate or take away from any other thought process but to allow yourself to have new possibilities encompassing the already existing options—then you allow those new neural pathways to open up and connect and reach to these other neural pathways. Then they can connect and fire together with them to open up new ideas and possibilities. That connection is a pretty loose connection at first until they fire several times, and then that possibility will open up in your mind, and new things will come to support that as a possibility. It opens up your whole mindset to something completely new that you hadn't imagined before.

All the connecting and supporting neural pathways will then connect to support a new way to look at something, a new way to be right. You get to keep your old way but you add onto the new neural pathways of what you're doing. You get to be more right. You're not only right with your current viewpoint based on the neural pathways that are now firing together, but you're even more right because you have additional neural pathways that will connect and open up new possibilities and open up more of your mind and your thinking. In the Philosophy of Possibility, scientists, doctors, critics, and researchers are merely reporters because what they do is observe facts, and report based on the available concepts to them at the time of their observations. That's why so often we hear about miracles. A miracle is something that happens that a doctor, scientist, specialist didn't think would happen. For instance, if a patient is suddenly cured of cancer—that's a miracle. Of course, the cancer which is out of control cell growth, could stop growing and destroying other cells just because the patient stopped eating something that was toxic and the cancer reversed. It could have even just been a change in stress. Yet what a doctor will do is observe cancer. In a space of the Philosophy of Possibility, doctors, scientists, and researchers are merely reporting the currently observable facts, analyzing them, making statistics out of them.

CHAPTER 17

Blind Faith in Authorities Over the Truth

"Blind Belief in authority is the greatest enemy of truth." –
Albert Einstein

At the age of fifteen, I was in business, successfully supplying general merchandise to retail stores with no business license. But, one of my customers, a big retail store I was selling to, required me to provide a proof of business license. So I went to the Vallejo Business Licensing office. I spoke to the counter person at the licensing department; and she said that I needed to be the legal age of eighteen years old to obtain a business license. I said, "I am conducting business without a license, that's not legal. I need a license." I asked to speak to the manager, Glen. He came to the counter extremely irritated. He repeated what was said.

I asked, "With all due respect, is that your policy?"

He said, "No, it's written in the codes."

My mind went to secret codes like in a 007 or Mission Impossible movie. I asked, "Codes, what are those?"

He told me that codes are agreements that the City Council agree on to manage the City.

Very nervous and anxious, I asked, "Can I see these codes please?"

"Yes," he said.

He brought out a four-inch binder. I spent four hours reading it. Then at the end of the binder in a tab that was labeled exceptions, I found, "If a person is under the age of eighteen the person does not have to pay for a business license." I jumped up, ran to the counter and showed it to Glen. He wrote me an E & A Imports business license. That was all I needed to provide to my customer and pick up a check. I ran out the door as fast as I could be, hoping that nothing would change.

The danger here is when the authority becomes considered as the truth rather than truth as the authority.

If I had not read for four hours and questioned the authority, it's possible that today I would not be in business. I get overwhelmed with emotion when I think about this pivotal moment in my life. That one authority could have change the direction of my life forever.

The city manager had gotten the truth completely wrong. Also, the written codes said that a business license is a tax to do business and not a contract. My life could be altered, but I had not submitted my trust to the authority over the truth. The danger here is when the authority becomes considered as the truth rather than truth as the authority.

What's more interesting to me is the authority of, let's say, the idea of the impossible.

Let's look at another viewpoint: when an authoritative figure has an opinion, judgment, criticism, or observation they make about you, that identifies and defines *who they are* and may not *necessarily* have anything to do with you whatsoever.

I'm not saying anything is true. I'm not here to tell you something is right or wrong. I'm not coming from that space. I'm not in authority. I don't plan to be. What's more interesting to me is the authority of, let's say, the idea of the impossible.

The hardest authority to overcome is you!

An encyclopedia from 1951 claimed it was impossible for man to go to the moon and back. Then the United States' Apollo 11 completed a mission landing 20 July 1969. There are countless other truths once thought impossible. There was a time when the "world was flat." The authorities said that the world was flat. It looked flat from their viewpoint, and that's what they declared. Physically, man couldn't run a four-minute mile, known as a four-minute barrier. Then came Roger Bannister in 1954 with 3:59.4. Now over 4500 people have done it with the current record held by Hicham El Guerrouj 3:43:13.

There was also a time when the authority said that the sun circled the earth. The possibility of being human is opening up the possibility of having things as they are, yet remaining open to the possibility that we're willing to give it up when something else may present itself.

The idea of possibility in the realm of authority and the truth is that truth can change as more possibility comes into the realm. You're broadening the idea of truth where authorities have less effect because you're able to see things as they are and not as you are told they are. If I told you the earth was flat today, you'd look at me and say, "No, it's not," and you'd feel certain about that. If I said that the sun rotated around the earth, you'd say, "You're wrong." However, if I said, "See, the interesting thing is the earth rotates

What you see to be "true" is not necessarily true.

around the sun, and the sun and the earth rotate around something else," then depending on where you observe something, your viewpoint changes the possibility of your truth. The hardest authority to overcome is you!

Truth from the area of possibility is a viewpoint, and the more viewpoints you can absorb, the more possibility you have for understanding more of the truth. You can look at a wall of a building and say, "Wow, there's a building there." Yet if you go behind the building and realize that it's just a wall that from front looks like a building, it's a façade like on a movie set and

The truth is a momentary experience; it evolves and is fluid and has lots of possibilities.

what's on the other side is empty space. Now we discover the truth that the wall is just a façade of what looks like a building. You have to observe it from the other side to see it as something different. What you see to be "true" is not necessarily true. Living in possibility is living in the question that what you see is what you see; yet it's possible that there can be many different possibilities for the truth.

What's true for you today is probably different to you than what was true for you when you were seven years old. What's true for you today, I would most definitely say, will be different

Possibility of truth juxtaposed to the authority of the truth.

than what's true for you a year from now. The attachment to the idea of truth itself can be a fixed idea. The truth is a momentary experience; it evolves and is fluid and has lots of possibilities. The possibility of what could be true for you is the question of what could be true. It's your question.

Now, this may sound like philosophical talk, yet it's not meant to. It's meant to open you up the idea of the possibility of truth juxtaposed to the authority of the truth. Because what we're looking for is the generation of truth that comes from within, open to the possibility of different viewpoints, which can change and evolve ideas, thoughts, feelings, and experiences that shape what's true for us now and allows the possibility of there being truth in ideas, thoughts, feelings, and experience.

CHAPTER 18

Create a Positive Identity in Crisis

Ludwig Wittgenstein, a philosopher and linguist, was born into a wealthy family where mathematics and philosophy carved the world into perfect logic defining the limitations of language. Throughout his life, his philosophical thought was to make life perfect, to show language in its perfection, to outlining what's possible in the language. Later on he realized and embraced that language wasn't only perfect structure, but included things that were imperfect that were just as important and perfect as the language he had. Concrete ideas like "handbag"—which we get an image of—was his early philosophy. Later, he pulled in the philosophy of things that don't pull up images in our mind—words like "perhaps," "seem," "idea," and "frustration"—yet would encompass more of the emotional and conceptual states of life as well. He encompassed both the specific and the conceptual so that he could bring together a life that is complete.

I see that conflict is just as important as agreement.

From my personal insight, I see that conflict is just as important as agreement. Disagreement is just as valuable, if not more valuable in some circumstances, than agreement. If you agree to things that you don't truthfully agree with, then you're not living within your language. You're out of integrity. Thus conflict in being is just as essential as no conflict.

It's important that you discuss life and push the boundaries. Pushing those boundaries can be a critical, violent force of disagreement. When you challenge the barriers of people's lives and your life, you end up with conflict. When you challenge who you are, you may see a violent conflict because this disagrees with who you are, not even separate from yourself, yet it's part of who you are. Who do you think you are? When you start to question that, you question everything that you are, and you start to go deep into a positive identity crisis.

This is a safe way to have an identity crisis by separating yourself from your identity so that you have more options and possibilities in life. The first stage is that you simply have an identity crisis to see that it is an identity and that you can pull away from it. Once you're able to pull away from your identity, thoughts, and self-image, you can turn around and start to challenge or disagree with the ideas of that identity. Doing this will take some of the life out of what you want to do—because the survival of identity is so important—but ask yourself this: Are you really the person you've always believed you are?

When has it taken some of the life out of what you want to do, because the survival of this identity is so important to be sure that you are the person you always believed you were? When has that identity drifted away from love, accomplishment, success, experience, friendship, and joy?

The first step in self-awareness is to have an identity crisis—to start looking at who you are and how you became that, but not because it matters how you became that, that's insignificant. It's just that you start to take a look at the pieces and the insights you can pull away from, and you're able to get an experience of being able to see how that identity was formed, further pulling you away from that identity, leading you to more options in life. You can choose differently because your IT, identity, ego, and self-image are not choosing for you; that's what you would normally do, yet that is not the real you.

An identity crisis enables you to pull away from your subconscious identity to gather this luminous enlightenment which starts to move in the direction that gives you more options and eventually, possibility. When you get past the options of the things that your ego, identity, or self-awareness wants you to be, you'll be in the realm of where you're moving in a direction where you're able to live in a question, and possibilities can come to you when you're looking at anything. You'll see the possibilities that are past options because you'll no longer be reflecting on an identity or the opposition to that identity. You're no longer looking to or against the group. You're no longer agreeing or disagreeing with mom and dad, or the family values, or the city you live in, or the country. You can be for or against these. It's giving you sort of an anchor point for your spirit, almost a grounding.

When has that identity drifted away from love, accomplishment, success, experience, friendship, and joy?

There's that sense of feeling attached to something, perhaps to our parents or where we live. There's a sense of a feeling grounded or of having value or attachment, but you're not more attached to those things than you think you are. You're dependent yet separate. When you live in possibility, you're able to fully experience those moments because you're not looking at whether you agree or disagree. That's an optional conversation. You're looking from a possibility. As long as you're acting from a place of agreeing or disagreeing, you're coming from

It's giving you sort of an anchor point for your spirit, almost a grounding.

ego or someone else's ego in an effort not to be dominated by another person or to dominate. Starve the ego and feed the possibilities!

Your ego is all about looking good, sounding clever, and being important and valuable. All those things are the essence of creating the survival of that ego, and that ego pushes to survive. There's something way past that ego—a life that's full, one that can be experienced because when you're in a set of options, you don't get to experience life to its fullest. How you experience life turns into a concrete idea or a concept of what you thought happened, which is limited to the language that you've articulated. That experience acts like a filter that puts you in a cage that you belong or are a part of. I say you belong because you put yourself there. No one else puts you in that cage. You have bought in or agree when IT suits you and when IT works for you and when IT helps you survive. Each time you do that, you end up deeper in a tighter cage that you put yourself in, and that's difficult to get out of.

Options close down directions and paths. Possibility opens them up.

When you're living in full possibility, you get a deeper, richer experience of life because it isn't based on past options of whether you agreed or didn't agree, or whether it fits in your jar. These concepts or ideas have to fit in your jar to further define your ego, support your self-image, and make you someone who is important, valid, looks good, or sounds smart in society. That is the essence of what you're pushing for when you're coming from that place of options or your identity. To live in the possibility is to open yourself completely. Options close down directions and paths. Possibility opens them up.

Your ego is all about looking good, sounding clever, and being important and valuable.

CHAPTER 19

Create and Live in Possibility

The Philosophy of Possibility allows you to notice the magnitude that the impact of the culture, family, nature, and past has on who you think you are. You must undercut all of that to graduate into the space of being what's possible. This is a complete opening beyond you as an individual, a name, thought, emotion, and an idea. It is you as a being, as a total possibility, a complete possibility, and all possibilities.

Living in this state of possibility takes commitment, dedication, responsibility, openness, and keeping yourself open to the possibility that life is. Here you are without fixed ideas or fixed concepts, and not living in delusion or illusion. Living in possibility means remaining open to ideas, concepts, and events that move you further in life, and able to make a declaration at any moment and step into being and a way of being.

Freeing Possibility

The freeing of the possibility is to be free from mind, body, and emotion. Those are common obstacles that obscure our thinking. Clearing your mind, emotions, and physical being allows you to be completely present in the space of nothing to create anything. The reason I say create is because creation coming off of something or in limited beliefs is not true creation.

True ultimate creation comes out of nowhere and nothing. It isn't a copy or derivative of something. It is organic and fresh. It has no price to pay to other authors or to other people or anything they acknowledge. If it is true creation, it gives you life. You feel so alive when you create something.

This is the arena of being able to create from a space of nothing. That is a total possibility, and you can live in that. Every day can be that way. You don't have to limit yourself. You don't have to buy into or agree with the limitations people put on you, or you put on yourself.

True ultimate creation comes out of nowhere and nothing

Limiting Potential

Your potential is limited when you operate from within a context, when you operate from a belief system, ideas, or a specific way of thinking such as a religion or an occupation. You can open up your true potential by letting go of those contexts. You can get to the space of nothing, to where not even time exists, such as days of the week, months, or years. The ultimate place is operating from the space of nothing, and getting back to nothing is a process. Eventually, you can be in the space of nothing immediately. There's no reason that you can't. There's nothing that would keep you from being there. So it's your toolbox or rule jar that will determine whether you can let yourself get to that space of nothing, let go of the chatter that goes on in your mind, and sit still.

Nothing is your mind's enemy.

To be in the space of nothing doesn't mean that you have to be sitting still. You could be running or walking.

In fact, the first thing is to identify, notice, and shatter the jar that limits you and takes apart those ideas and specific dogmas. Begin by taking apart those fixed concepts using questioning, looking inside yourself, accepting it for what it is, and letting it go. Let it resolve through the process of getting, seeing, and acknowledging so it's not something that you're going to argue or fight with. When you try to get in the space of nothing, and I emphasize the word *try*, you find yourself fighting the fact that you can get to nothing. Your mind is trying to survive. Nothing is your mind's enemy. Getting to the space of nothing is like not surviving. It's like not being. Your mind is constantly trying to be right and be something, like looking good, avoiding looking bad, etc. Your mind is looking for these strategies constantly, and it fights for them. You get to choose, and your choices give it power. So in getting back to nothing, your mind is going to fight like hell, and it's going to pull up everything it possibly can to survive and justify its existence, and that is where you're limiting your potential. It starts and it ends in the mind.

CHAPTER 20

Being Unreasonable

People tend to make over-generalized statements about people, cultures, things, religions, or mostly themselves. They use disabling, minimizing statements that are incomplete, not impeccably stated, and lack accuracy. Here is a perfect example: When I was talking to a loved one, I stated, "I'm soft." I was generalizing myself because I thought I could do a better job in a negotiation.

She said, "You know, you're not soft. Stop! You're intuitive and more accurately sensitive. You're very strong, passionate; go after what you want and stand up for it, and people. You're very far from being a pushover. You're flexible, yet you're intuitively sensitive and strong at the same time."

She had a point. With some people, I can sensitively adjust myself to be warm, friendly, and soft, and I had those two exactly pieced together. I felt that I was soft. I felt that people were pushing me around. That was not the case. As she pointed out, when people try to push me over, I'm sensitive to that. I get upset, angry and put a stop to it. Just by her taking me past the generalization of what it is to be "soft"—by looking at it and relooking at it and redefining it, I made a distinction there between those two. I was able to realize that

I had myself contained in a jar called, "I'm soft." which, up until that examination, was a jar I was unaware of.

I'm an entrepreneur. I go out there and go after it. I take on the battles. I have taken on some powerful people. I've taken on government entities. I've taken on Fortune 500 & 100 companies, toe to toe. Little ole' me has taken on Wall Street companies that hired nationally recognized law firms. They might have deep pockets and be beating the crap out of me, yet I can sure fight back; I just didn't give up. I know I'm not a pushover. I know I'm not soft, yet I had myself in that distinction until she unraveled that and said, "You know what? You're sensitive. You're not soft." I have beaten a billionaire and Tooele County.

Conditions don't last forever.

What kind of jar do you live in? If you define or label yourself with general statements, like that you're soft, then what happens is you feel and think soft. You will make your decisions based on being "soft" but you are strong. You can get your wants and needs and still be sensitive and compassionate for other people. Have empathy for them, not sympathy. You can feel for their situation, and not feel sorry for them. That's a big distinction. I feel for people's situations, and I have empathy. I don't feel sorry for them. Conditions don't last forever. You can change your situation and condition. You can move forward.

If you want to live like other people don't, you should be willing to put in what other people won't.

You can open your jar wider. Imagine your life being a little studio. You expand your life so that you can't fit all your furniture in the studio; you can't fit all your life in with your kids and your mate. You can move into a mansion, yet you have to open your jar to something that would support the thoughts and actions that represent being in a mansion. One way to do that is by creating multiple revenue streams from multiple businesses and investments. You may have to work harder than most people are willing to work. If you want to live like other people *don't*, you should be willing to put in what other people *won't*. You've got to commit. You've got to go for it. That means coming out of your jar you're living in right now. Whatever constraints you have, you're living in them right now.

I challenge you to realize there's no jar that will contain you.

Everything you have is a result of everything you believe and everything you put yourself into. You're exactly where you should be, where you want to be, where you ought to be, and where you could be. It's all by your design. It's all by your design and what you're comfortable with within your jar.

I challenge you to break out of your jar. I challenge you to realize there's no jar that will contain you. They'll try to confine you to a jar, put you in a jar, take you to a jar, secure you in a jar, give you ideas in a jar, generalize you into a jar. I say, "You can't build a big enough jar for me." You are truly limited by your thoughts, ideas, and thinking process. How big are your ideas? How big are your thoughts?

You have to be completely unreasonable.

When you have a big idea, and you talk yourself out of it because of all your rules, you're not thinking big enough. Your jar is smaller because your thoughts are smaller, or because you invalidate those thoughts. To have a bigger jar, you must have bigger ideas, which means you have to have fewer constraints on your ideas, and you have to go for it. You get to the point where you must become unreasonable with yourself and with other people. You have to be completely unreasonable. I tell you that because you've got to be unreasonable with yourself as well. You've got to go outside of reasonable to achieve extraordinary results, which will only be extraordinary to you today. Tomorrow, that will be ordinary, and you'll be looking to grow further.

When you were a baby, it was extraordinary to see other people walk. It was unreasonable to think you could walk. However, you kept trying, trying, and eventually you started walking. Today you walk without even thinking about it. You don't even appreciate it unless you see somebody who can't walk. You are taking walking for granted because it is an ordinary thing to you.

You've got to go outside of reasonable to achieve extraordinary results

Get out of your constraints and the reasons you give yourself for why you do what you do, how you do it, when you should do it, and with whom you should do it. Those are all reasons. You're logical within your constraints, within your rules, within the rules that you grew up with, whether it's your mom's programming, your teacher's programming, or your culture's programming. You hear all kinds of crazy horrible things that happen to people. This is your programming at work. Be afraid. Be scared. These are the buttons that capture your attention. Those are the constraints you have and create.

To get outside, you have to do things that you consider aren't reasonable. They have to be outside of reason. Your jar needs to be unreasonable. When what you thought was extraordinary becomes ordinary, then you take the next step. The key is that you get out of the struggle, the survival, the just-over-broke. Find adventure and fun. Help your company grow, help whatever you're into grow. Move in a positive direction. Align with people who care about you and want to see you move ahead and succeed. I know you think that's not reasonable, but this isn't about being reasonable. It's about being unreasonable. Challenge yourself every day. Challenge your ideas. Challenge your thoughts. Know that it's possible even if it's unreasonable. Believe that it can be done. Take the step forward and move in the direction of achieving what you want to achieve, how you want to achieve, when you want to achieve. Make those declarations and goals. Write them down. Put yourself out there.

Know that it's possible even if it's unreasonable.

Be at risk. Have goals that are completely unreasonable. Anybody can do what's reasonable. In your sleep, you can do what's reasonable—and most people are asleep in their daily life. They are asleep in their mundane life with their mundane spouse, in their mundane car, doing their mundane job, with their mundane lifestyle. They go through mundane life all the way to death. They have a mundane routine because it's safe. That's not living. Sure, you can do that. Maybe there isn't anything wrong with it. It's just not the life I choose. If you want to be mundane, be mundane. If you're comfortable being mundane, then be comfortable.

Choose it and own it.

Choose it and own it. If you're reading this book or listening to this on audio, it's because you're looking for a new life. If you want an extraordinary life, be unreasonable. Don't let the jar you're in contain you, then build a bigger jar. As soon as you see a jar, you can also see what's outside of that jar. You can expand it and grow it in many different ways because you define it.

Be unreasonable.

CHAPTER 21

Reality of Agreements

An exchange of money is an example of an agreement of the simplest and most basic kind. When an agreement is made, and you are supposed to receive payment, you say, "We have an agreement, and I haven't received the money that was promised. When will I get it?" This is a simple question. Nothing personal, and nothing added. There's no excuse, reason, or justification for me asking.

If you let it get personal, the agreement shifts. If you say, "I need the money," then you set yourself up to have to justify it, and the "need" of course is a disempowering position and belief. It clouds the question. It gives the question the opportunity to turn ugly. It's now personal both for you and for them. If they decide, "Well, you don't need the money," then you'll just look like a mean, uncompassionate person by adding emotional clutter to it. The focus now is off of the agreement and on whether you *need* the money or not.

When we add things to an agreement and make it personal, we are disempowered and create an upset on the other side as well. It's important that we stay specific and use impeccable language for what it is that we want or are doing. If you tell a story, and you give reasons for consequences in your life that will happen by not receiving the money, the other person will start to evaluate any consequences and decide whether or not they can live with them. Now you're completely off of the original agreement. How does this show up in your life, not just with money but any agreement?

When agreements are made and kept, trust is developed, and growth can happen by keeping agreements. That's what people, investors, and friends are looking for. They're looking for people who make commitments and fulfill agreements.

When agreements are made and kept, trust is developed, and growth can happen by keeping agreements.

The agreements can be modified. If you're not willing to modify an agreement when life happens, you're arguing with reality. So again, you're going to experience disempowerment. You want to create a situation where you can get the result you're looking for.

CHAPTER 22

The Experience of Love

Is being happily married an oxymoron? Absolutely not, if you love from possibility. The love that we first experience when we "fall in love" is perfect. Everything is possible, and life is completely turned on. The problem occurs when love becomes routine, common, and obligated. We fall out of *"experience"* into a different love: the *"concept of love."* When the experience of love turns into the concept of love, we look to match it up to our unconscious model of love. For me, my unconscious model was what I observed from my mother who did the laundry, cooked, cheered on my father, listened to his concerns, and complimented his hard work. Every few months they had a big fight of some misunderstanding blown completely out of proportion, but then they made up and were madly in love again. Until I discovered possibility, I had not examined love if a woman did not do laundry, cook, cheer me on, and listen to me. Reinforcement of love was for me having a misunderstanding with my partner who showed me that passion and commitment, and would allow me to experience love. When it matched, I allowed myself to love.

We fall out of "experience" into a different love: the "concept of love."

117

Love from possibility doesn't have the options attached to it that you allow yourself to experience love. This is love from possibilities. It's not from any fixed idea or any understanding or any expression of love, but it's the question of love—the idea that could be in the space that is love. There are new and different possibilities for love, possibilities that I haven't opened myself up to yet. It's the constant search to discover ways to experience love in the moment with no attachment to the past, future or any expectation.

What I know about love, what I've learned about love, and what my parents and all the relationships have taught me about love, are only a beginning. We have to divorce those fixed ideas to live in the possibility, the question, and opening that love is. When you come from the question of love, you're living in the idea that there's the possibility of love—loving in new ways, in different ways, in more expressive ways. You open up a space that enables you to love more flowingly and accept experiences. You allow yourself to get past difficulties, misunderstandings, fixed concepts, and ideas that you have about love, that you have to match up for you to experience love.

> **It's the constant search to discover ways to experience love in the moment with no attachment to the past, future or any expectation.**

We can experience, give and generate love without having to first match up to our concept of what we expect love to be. You can experience love from the space of its possibility, not a fixed idea, not a decision. This is a space of loving, and you get to "un-know" love; the loving you express every day in your current relationship. To get the experience of "un-knowing" love is like an idea when you first started out your relationship. You knew nothing about this person. The possibility of love was open and great. Life was turned on, anything was possible with this person, and you were excited.

Relationship experts have found that when you get comfortable in the relationship and its routine, you fall into a model of what you "expect" in a relationship. When your loved one expresses herself/himself in the pattern that meets your expectation, then you allow yourself to experience love. This is the concept you have about love. If your loved one matches up to your concept about love, then you will experience love. That's love from options, conditions, and circumstances—not experiential love.

Experiential love, the expression of love from possibility, is the space of complete openness and vulnerability of experiencing love. This allows love to flow into you in all its different ways. There are many people trying to love you right now, yet you have no idea they have been trying to love you. There are so many expressions of love, yet you don't experience love as they express it. If they do not match up with your expectation or concept of love, your belief about love, your option about love, then guess what? You don't experience love that a person has for you.

We can experience, give and generate love without having to first match up to our concept of what we expect love to be.

Some people express love with anger. Some people express love with excitement and enthusiasm. Some people express love from a space of fear, or of vulnerability. If you don't look at where this expression of love is coming from, you won't get the idea that

Experiential love, the expression of love from possibility, is the space of complete openness and vulnerability of experiencing love.

they're coming from the space of love. Instead, you get the idea that they're coming from some other space because that doesn't match up with the feeling that you express when you accept the idea that this person loves you.

My stepfather, who raised me, loved me, and most of the time he loved me from a very angry state. He was angry, and he yelled at me a lot. I experienced love from a state of somebody yelling at me, and I had many relationships that unless they yelled, I didn't know whether somebody cared about me or not. I believed care equaled anger. I'm not saying that's functional or dysfunctional, yet it limited me to the options through which I had experienced love.

CHAPTER 23

Seeing Possibility

Before I start this chapter I want do a quick exercise. Please read this sentence: "FINISHED FILES ARE THE RESULT OF YEARS OF SCIENTIFIC RESEARCH MERGERED WITH THE EXPERIENCE OF MANY YEARS." Now go back and count the number of F's in the sentence. I have done this test with many people and usually 50 percent of people see 3 F's. There are 6 F's, look again at it. Did you count the F in the word "of"? There are 6 F's. Interesting isn't it. Seeing from possibility is seeing the F's in life.

Were physically wired not to see, hear or feel all that is possible.

Don't feel bad. Were physically wired not to see, hear or feel all that is possible. We have what is called Reticular Activating System (RAS) or extra-thalamic control modulatory system. It is a biological set of connected nuclei in the brains of vertebrates that is responsible for regulating wakefulness and sleep-wake transitions. As its name implies, its most influential component is the reticular formation. This is the portal through which nearly all information enters the brain. It acts like a filter between our conscious and our subconscious mind. This system plays a major role in your ability to achieve goals. There is so much data coming in that it filters it for us. Otherwise we probably could not focus.

The problem with this is it *filters*, throwing out information. Information that could be otherwise, very useful. There is a scene in Superman where they show what it would look like if you didn't have this filter (RAS). They show Superman in a crowd and he begins to hear all the conversations people are having at once making it impossible to comprehend.

Start by opening up and giving yourself new eyes from this viewpoint to experience overriding this system.

Start by opening up and giving yourself new eyes from this viewpoint to experience overriding this system. Do you think you see what is there or do you see what you want to see!? Have you ever taken an inkblot test? You say what you see in the ink, and it builds your personal context or lens from what you say you see. Seeing from possibility, however, is seeing and *observing* what you see and listening to your thoughts yet not *being* your thoughts. You would observe what you're seeing and listening to your feelings, yet not be your feelings. Seeing and experiencing your body, yet not being your body. When you see from possibility, you're open to seeing more of what's there to see. That's the key: opening your eyes and seeing what is there, what's *really* there. Not what you think is there, not what you feel is there, or what your body experiences as there but what actually is there.

We see in "the question" from possibility. What am I not seeing? What could be there? What might be there? What is possible to be there? The longer you sit at that moment, the longer you avoid assumption and contextual jar thinking, which is all experiences you've had in life, your history, your upsets all coming into the present moment. This is clouding the moment with the past, so you don't see what's there. This is an opportunity to see for the first time in your life.

I'd like you to do an exercise: Walk around a room and just look at people and things. Look at individuals and things from the space of possibility.

When we are looking at people—objectifying, classifying and judging them—we close down any space for their being. To open up space, we come from a place of possibility to be an opening, not a defining, but an *undefining* of the moment to see new distinctions, realities, and possibilities. That's truly seeing! Seeing from the perspective of possibility opens us up to the idea that we can see what's there. When you experience what I'm talking about, experiencing actual space, you'll notice the person who's talking to you, and you'll be able to be who you are, where you are and when you are. You're not protecting what was done in the past or defending how you're dressed or explaining your hairstyle. They're giving you space, looking for the acceptance of what is or what they see, accepting that space, accepting what is there.

I'm not saying that you're taking and agreeing with it, not at all. I'm saying be open to the space of accepting what you can see and looking to accept more of what is there. You open up the space in order to really see not only with your eyes, thoughts, feelings, body, heart, and ideas or concepts about a person, not only with these limitations that you have about what you think you see.

CHAPTER 24

Hearing from Possibility

Before I discovered possibility, I had the basic context that "I already knew." For example, when a person began to talk, I quickly assessed the goal or outcome of what they were about to say. I heard what I wanted to hear from the option "I already knew everything." I would cut them off and respond with "I know ... oh, what were you saying?" I had been operating from the space that I had to be right about the fact "I knew." Imagine trying to explain something to me and with two words I wouldn't be listening to you anymore, although I thought I was listening. The IT already heard what it wanted to hear, quickly jarred it, and framed it.

What are you already listening for? What jars are you constantly looking to fill to be right about?

We're going to analyze different things that we hear until we interpret what we have heard so that we can discover what it is that hearing with possibility allows us to do. I want you to think about what happens when you hear the voice of someone you care about. What's your experience when they talk? I want you to feel when you hear their voice talking to you. I want you to experience your body when they are talking to you, and I want you to experience the judgments you make about the way they talk. Look at the judgments you made about them from the sound, rhythm, and the intonation of their voice. Look at the ideas you have about them, the context you're putting them in, the lens that you're looking at them from.

It's natural for human beings to judge others. Our minds have a tendency to try to define, explain, reason, and justify to survive. Survival is about defining things. Survival is certainty and uncertainty is death.

Your brain is coming from a space of a need to be right about everything, right about something, right in the face of being completely out of whack. It has a desire to be right regardless if it's wrong. The brain's ultimate survival equals being right. "I am right." To be wrong is to be dead. Some people have a preconceived concept that they're wrong about everything, so they look to be wrong about something so they can be right about the fact that they're wrong.

Survival is certainty and uncertainty is death.

Don't think that this is escapable.

It's not.

Hearing others through possibility means hearing completely without judgment, emotion, thought, or physical interruption. "Possibility hearing" is hearing the question. It's the experience of hearing openly in a question. Don't you ever notice that sometimes what you hear isn't as important as what you don't hear? Imagine you're listening to a sales presentation about something you would love to do, like take a cruise around the world. What you hear is wonderful, yet what you do not hear could be tragic, especially after you've saved and spent all your money. Listening to what is not said is as important as what is said, or could be said. We hear all the beautiful things, yet what are we not told? What's missing? Why would it be missing?

Those are options of hearing and not hearing, and this is not about option-thinking. When you hear something, try to figure out what you're not hearing. Hearing in possibility means you're open, and you allow your mind, feelings, and body to free-flow without getting stuck. You can get stuck by romanticizing, exaggerating, and repeating your set of options. Be open to letting each moment be a moment in itself and experiencing what you're undergoing in the moment, listening to your thoughts, not being your thoughts, or hearing your feelings. This is an opening.

CHAPTER 25

Possibility of Thinking

Possibility and Opportunity thinking is the highest level of intelligence. It's focused on the ability to observe from a separate position from the mind. Allow the space to hold two, or several, opposing and supporting ideas in the mind at the same time. Thinking from the realm of possibility is a different kind of thinking than thinking from options or opinions. Normally, what people are accustomed to is that they look at something and immediately have an opinion about it. That's the essence of a snap judgment, understanding, reason, assumption, and critical impression about something. That is called an *opinion*: option-thinking.

Thinking from the possibility is thinking from the idea that you'll look at something and allow several thoughts into your mind. Then you'll question or take a look at the thoughts from that perspective. You'll look at what you are and not be thinking about something, what

Allow the space to hold two, or several, opposing and supporting ideas in the mind at the same time.

you might be thinking about it for, and what purpose it serves. Look at the idea of something from different perspectives, such as how someone else might think about that, or how you might think somebody might think about that, or how it may be, or what its perspective may be. You'll look at the question of something that you don't know about a particular thing, and you'll allow that thinking-ness that's there to sit in the mystery of the experience of being with something long enough to have new distinctions, categories, and understandings about what you're looking at. It almost takes a stop-pause moment to be open to thinking about what's there for you as opposed to a snap judgment or opinion about something.

The powerfulness of possibility and possibility thinking requires practice and actual time spent thinking about something. It's an opening to being in the perspective of thinking in a broader, more open, allowing way, and see-

When you live in possibility, you open up your life.

ing things as they are. It's about being okay with your thoughts to understand new perspectives, new ways of looking at that or new ways of thinking about that. That is the essence of possibility thinking.

When you live in possibility, you open up your life. *You* open up. I want to open your eyes, open your ears, open your heart, open your expression, open the you that is bigger than your thoughts, your feelings and your body. That is the possible you.

CHAPTER 26

Key Human Traps

When we feel a need to be dominant or that we are being dominated, we fall away from possibility and into the trap of options. One trap is the need to be *right or avoid being wrong*. When you're working hard on trying to be right, your past is trying to get reinforcement or agreement with past events. Moments of your past cast shadows into the present. They capture you in the trap of options and run you off the present moment road. These two traps keep you from seeing, hearing, loving, and being with what is right in front of you. When you're fighting to be right, you put yourself in a situation of being malleable and controllable. You can be easily manipulated. You can be dominated, so you're limiting your possibility and living in the options. When you're choosing to be right or avoid being wrong, and dominate or avoid domination, you're stuck in the trap that limits you and gets you stuck in the options.

Another trap is the need to look good or avoid looking bad. When you come from the place of wanting to look good or avoiding looking bad in front of others, such as being embarrassed,

Moments of your past cast shadows into the present.

it will throw you off the course of possibility. These traps will send you in the direction of fear, and you'll avoid doing things for the fear of looking bad, being dominated, or being wrong. It is like a gravitational pull propelled by the intoxication of being dominating, right, or good. Things that are outside the realm of what is the ultimate best for you will begin to surface and surround you. These traps are like a drug to the mind. These are the things to be cognizant of when you're operating in the space of possibility. These motivators are the core ones that will lead you into the trap: being right, looking good, dominating others, or avoiding domination, being wrong, or looking bad.

Three more traps are the need to evaluate, invalidate, and validate. These three can separate people from their possibility. This is a different way to look at being right, looking good, and dominating. You're not in the possibility if you're in any of those human traps.

You are in a wanting trap when you say you "want" something. This statement is telling your subconscious mind that: "You don't have it." "You can't have it." "You won't have it." That stains your mind and keeps you from having it. It puts you on the outside of the "having." What we want is one of the problems associated with

> **These motivators are the core ones that will lead you into the trap: being right, looking good, dominating others, or avoiding domination, being wrong, or looking bad.**

making the statement of wanting something. Wanting something is the perfect way to guarantee that you'll probably never get it. Wanting to be happy makes being happy a chase that is unobtainable. You think something will make you happy when you get it, but it won't happen from the place of wanting.

So what is the solution? Generating happiness and creating happiness is the way to be happy. It's that simple. You're inside of happy as opposed to being outside of happy. Instead of looking at happiness and wanting it, when you are happy, you'll see everybody that's happy, and it feels normal to be happy. If you're not happy, you'll be upset that they are happy and you're not. Wanting is not having. It's a "romantic sensation" of embellishing what you don't have. Commit to coming from the creation and generation that you already have everything you desire. You're generating that, and you're vibrating at that level, and your thinking, being, emotion, and body will follow to support it. Like magic, it will become true. Create it, generate it.

When you tell yourself that you have or "need" to do something a trap of negative energy emerges, pushes you down, and pulls you back from actually doing it. It makes the effort to do it that much harder. It takes more effort to do something that you "have to do" or you "need to do" than something you "committed to doing" and you "get to do." It's just your conversation that directs the direction of your thought patterns.

Wanting is not having. It's a "romantic sensation" of embellishing what you don't have.

It's very different when you come from the place where you commit to doing something, and you get to do something. You communicate to other people when you say that you are committed to doing something, and when you get to do it, you're excited about it. The idea that they'll hand it to you and *let* you do it is a lot more possible than if you tell them that you *have* to do it, and you need to do it, which comes from a place of duty, obligation, and guilt. It's a negative energy that's going to pull you down. Your physical frequency level will be so low that you're not going to be able actually to get it done because you'll be fighting with it. For example, statements like: you have to get something; you need to get something. These statements will be the last thing you do behind your statement of committing, and getting something.

everything is a "get to" and you're committed to getting things done.

So remember, everything is a "get to" and you're committed to getting things done.

Notice the language difference between "I need" and "I commit." "I need" can mean you're a victim, and it's got to happen to you, and you have to handle it so that you can grow. "I am committed" invites the opportunity to learn something, grow, and experience something different.

"I am committed" invites the opportunity to learn something, grow, and experience something different.

CHAPTER 27

Reach People by Conquering Suppression

Easy communication is a key indicator that people living in possibility doesn't have a lot of suppression in their world. Communication shows that their reach is extensive, meaning they're reaching out to people on a constant basis and excited to talk to people. That means their suppression of options is pretty low, and their expectation about the outcome of communicating with individuals is pretty high. They can appear pretty fearless. Clear communication is the foundation for success.

For instance, if you look at kids living more for what's possible than what's not, you'll see that their suppression is low. They haven't had a lot of negatives or losses in their lives. As a result of that, they reach, reach, reach, reach. They're happy. One of the biggest keys to being successful is being able to reach on a constant basis. To grow a business, it requires reaching out to people and providing either products or services.

Clear communication is the foundation for success.

If someone's reach is low, they tend to be heavily suppressed because of the negative experiences in their lives, so they are withdrawing.

Let's say you know that every time you get a call from a particular individual, it's going to be about money. You don't want to talk about money, and you aren't going to give any money, so you completely withdraw from communicating with this person. You know that the logic of that individual just won't accept what the reality is: you don't want to discuss money, and yet that person continues to persist talking about money. So you withdraw and completely shut down from further communication with that person. It stops and suppresses the entire flow of communication. To justify this, instead of saying it's about money, you will come up with other justifications and excuses for why you're no longer communicating with that person.

Notice what is suppressing you so you lift your suppression, and you'll live a fuller, happier life with lots of people in it. Your subjective justification narrows the facts and explains why you conform to those facts. It's almost impossible when believing in the possibility, to justify anything. This doesn't stop us much from trying to justify. It's so culturally important that you strategize on making up your justifications that you are going to be ultimately conforming to so that you can effectively sell the stories to others and yourself about why you don't have what you wanted.

Many times, a justification starts out with the question: "Why did you do that?" The question invites us into a subjective explanation justifying the objective facts, which ultimately ends up in a dwindling spiral. I think what's happening that opposes possibility is someone asking why they want to know whether you acted purposefully or unintentionally to screw up.

However, if it wasn't your intention, and it wasn't purposefully done, and it justifies your actions, there's a sense of comfort you get with the theme, "Okay great. He wasn't late on purpose. He wasn't late because he didn't intend to be on time. He intended to be on time, yet there was an accident, and so he feels better because he has an excuse for being late. The fact is he was still late."

The relationship can suffer if justification replaces truth. Rather than going to justification, it's possible to keep the relationship pretty clean and come from a space of "Yes. I was late, and I won't be late again. I'll make a better effort to be on time than I made this time. I'll prepare better to be here on time. Please accept my apology for taking up your time and causing you to have to wait for me." That would be pretty clean communication. Or to simply say, "It wasn't my intention to be late. I miscalculated, I won't do it again. I hope that you trust that I'll be here on time next time, and I completely apologize for being late." This is a better way to handle broken agreements. To justify and make up excuses only makes it worse than it already is.

In essence, people are looking for a commitment and if it was broken to reaffirm that commitment and also just that it wasn't your intention to break the commitment: "It wasn't my intention to break the commitment. I'll make a better effort, and I'll be here on time next time." The why is irrelevant at that point because you answered the question, which is the underlying assumption of whatever conversation is going on underneath.

CHAPTER 28

Choose to Risk Making Mistakes

To make the change, you need to put yourself out there and at risk and make as many mistakes as possible. Through reflection and sharing, you can begin to understand from your mistakes that you are not wrong, but there may be different workable choices. You can learn to resist the temptation of conformity and truly experience what's true for you. You can make the shift in yourself to move in the direction to get what it is that you want to get by putting yourself at risk.

It's time to take a solid look at your stories, justifications, reasons, and excuses so that you can process them in a way that you can see yourself and how you play the game of life. You cannot conform to the idea of the group, yet rather look at your truth, make up your mind and be responsible for your experience.

Part Four

POSSIBILITY IN PRACTICE

CHAPTER 29

The Art of Understanding

In the Philosophy of Possibility, understanding is an art not a science. Understanding is the ability to artfully fill in the gaps and figure stuff out. You need to understand creatively what somebody means when they say something—what they mean or what they want. There is an art of understanding another person's language and their writing style. This art of judging or figuring out encompasses what key points that are important to a person, what points they are establishing, what they prove right or wrong, what evidence or data are they using to understand, what it is that they are saying, and what's genuine. This is the art of understanding.

There's an art to language and understanding.

Don't take people literally. Most people don't even know the words that they're using and their definitions. Many people use words because they sound correct in a specific sentence or a phrase. Also, people are mimicking or copying much of their language and know their speaking styles and how they speak. They'll put words together that sound a certain way even though it can mean something completely different.

There's an art to language and understanding. Even when what you say is literal and specific and has an exact meaning, it can be interpreted or understood by people to mean something completely different. The more creative, intuitive and inquisitive you are about what somebody is saying, the better understanding you get of what they are saying or what they mean.

Imagine that many words used in their conversations are words that have invented wrong or incorrect definition. For example, the word "of" has seventeen definitions, "the" has fourteen definitions. Many definitions are enforced by family, school and work.

Now, let's consider for a moment that we are trying to communicate with each other, but we don't even have the same common agreement about the words we are using to communicate concepts to each other. You can find that many who speak English as a second language have a better understanding of the words' definitions and their uses in English language than someone whose first language is English. This is because second language individuals looked up the words and their uses in language, while someone who grew up with the language will mimic language thinking they already know the definition of the word. However, a native speaker will have a stronger understanding of slang and expressions from our language. For example, "He nailed it." "You wowed me."

CHAPTER 30

The Purpose of Self Discovery

What are your underlying concepts of self, about who and what you are? Say, for instance, that you'd answer that question with, "I'm a black man from the Bronx." Once you identify yourself as those distinctions, you have a subscribed set of options. Your options are that you're a man (which is another set of options) who is from the Bronx (which has its full set of options). When you say you're a black man from the Bronx, you have further limited your options if you're acting outside of that identity.

If you say you're a Christian black man from the Bronx, I say as a possibility that you have even more limited set of options. If you say you're a married Christian black man from the Bronx, you have even more limited set of options. If you say you're a married, black, Christian man with kids, who lives in the Bronx, I say you have even more limited options. If you say that you are a poor black man with kids, married who lives in the Bronx, I say you have limited yourself even further—not as a possibility, not like the truth, not like I want you to believe it.

Let me use another example: What if someone identifies himself or herself as being fat? I've never met a person who is fat. Yes, I've met people who carry extra weight on their bodies, yet you are not your body. So you are not fat, even if you self-identify as such because of the extra weight. Remember that even anorexics can see themselves as fat when they look in the mirror. They identify as being fat, even though they're not.

The reality is that if you identify as "fat," then you are living with limited options created by your past, and by the justifications and excuses you've made to explain your weight. The problem here is that you may have to give up who you think you are to get rid of the fat on your body. You have to transcend the belief that fat is your identity to seek the realm of possibility to be fit.

If I can reach it, I can have it.

I want you to understand your attachment to yourself, the idea of yourself and your thinking. I'm not saying this like it's true. I'm saying to look at it from the space of possibility. What possibilities do you have when you identify yourself as those things? What happens?

When you subscribe to an idea or a self that you limit, if you're attached to that, then you have a set of options. If you're detached from that, I say you still have a set of options, but not a possibility. If you're living from space and coming from possibility, then you can truly come from a place where everything is possible, and nothing is out of reach.

I want to discuss this thing called reach; what you can reach, what you can have, and what you can't have. It's pretty simple. I asked a kid. I was trying to figure out what I can have, saying, "God, I want to figure out how to help people get what they want." I found it frustrating, when a five-year-old sat there while I'm talking, and the kid looked at me and said, "Well, if I want candy and if I can reach it, I can have it."

The idea is profound if you think about it. Just look at it from a kid's perspective; without thinking, options and limitations, such as: You can't have candy; you're on a diet; it's out of reach; it's somebody else's candy.

Forget all those options and rules. A five-year-old kid looks at something from his perspective: "If I can reach it, I can have it," which is why you can find so many three-to-five-year-olds that devour anything they can reach. They understand from an early age that if they can reach something, they can have it. It's only through domestication that we're told about the rules, and we are confined in our jar and our present set of options.

For instance, when the options are that you're a married man with kids, black, poor, and lives on 46th Street in the Bronx, your conclusion is that you can't have more money. But you might be able to reach it. It might be as simple as walking down the road, and you reach out to somebody who has millions. Give him/her enough value in his/her life, work or the world to be fairly compensated so you can get out of being poor. You could create a situation like that if you accept your options, however, you may not even try.

Let's talk about creation. True creation comes from nothing. This should tell you something very important: If you want to invent/reinvent yourself, you've got to come from nothing. That's possibility. When you come from a preset list of options, there is no creation. There are only choices and options, not possibilities. Possibility, creating from nothing, is something you can extract from everywhere, and anything comes into being.

Take, for example, Steve Jobs. Maybe you like him, maybe you don't. Maybe you despise him, and maybe you don't. That's not the point because I'm not here to make him a hero. I think about Jobs as a true creator. When he created the iPod, people couldn't get the idea that you can have a thousand songs in something that is smaller than a deck of cards in your pocket. He was creating from nothing, from the space of something that hadn't been done yet. People could not understand how that could be possible. He looked at it from a completely different space. If he was going to capitalize on this market, he had to create a new way of looking at music. He had to create from nowhere a new model of understanding about the value that we place on music and how it's delivered.

That was not an easy goal because those concepts were violently countered. Jobs stood. He took a stand for music and its possibility of reshaping the agreements with the music industry in such a way that it has revolutionized and changed the standard of music creation, distribution, and fulfillment in our lives. The same happened with the first all-digital movie, *Toy Story*, which was another revolution of its kind created by Jobs. That was the first all-digital animation movie. The movie made box office history. Jobs pushed out the iPhone that integrated many devices and completely reinvented what was possible with a mobile phone.

It wasn't about taking the preset list of options, like so many other competitors do, and taking those sets of options and integrating them and trying to make the next better mousetrap. Jobs created something that wasn't even a mousetrap, although it still caught mice, so to speak. We have people who have created without the rules and not from the options in place, but from possibility. When you pioneer industries, there is an enormous reward.

When you let go of the precepts in your life, when you let go of your opinion of life, and you're open to creating from nothing, your life from possibility is limitless. Your life from the set of options is confined to your jar, to the space that others confine you to. The self-identity is before the part that is possible, the part before you think, the part before you feel. The self-identity always justifies, explains, reasons, and makes up stories for behavior that holds you back. It's exhausting making sure this identity stays intact, and these options are made available because these are your comfort zones.

What I'm saying to you is that the "you" who existed before

thinking, feeling, or your body, is possible. It is the essence of possibility. For me to give that part of you a name is to immediately ruin the experience of it. If I try to distinguish that and give it a name, it limits it to options. Here I am trying to speak to you about something that is unnamable. It's nonsense. I shouldn't even describe it as possible because I'm talking about the idea of complete possibility.

> **If I try to distinguish that and give it a name, it limits it to options.**

Being in the space of complete possibility means that you can see your self-image and have or not have a self-image and not be attached or detached to it. It's just an image. "Okay, I hear you. I feel you. I get it. Not attached to it, not detached to it." You can have a thought and look at your thought, and say, "Hey, thank you for sharing. Checking stuff out, analyzing it, processing it, dissecting it scientifically, acknowledging with a simple thank-you. I appreciate your input, yet I am not my mind. I am not my feeling. I am not my body or image or self-projection."

> **Who were you before you were who you are?**

That's what I want you to be. I'm not saying I'm right. I'm not saying whether to agree or disagree. This isn't an answer; it is an opening, an invitation to the possibility of you, the true possibility of you. You before thought, feeling, self-image, parents who gave you your body or, however, you got your name, before that. Who were you before you were who you are? If you're so attached to who you are or so detached in trying not to be who you are, I invite you to be with that for a moment and get the idea that there might not be another possibility. An invitation, an opening up to your true self—the true you.

CHAPTER 31

Inner Restriction and Conscious Disagreement

The inner restriction is an internal feeling or thought that holds you back. It's your inner restraint based on your thinking. For example, it might be the concern of another person who might judge or think badly about you. In most cases, the inner restriction you put on yourself isn't even real and wouldn't even affect or influence the person who's observing it.

We also have an inner restriction based on our upbringing, belief system, friends, church, family and social groups. All these mentioned and more have influence that impacts your decision to do something or not. Often restrictions are expressed internally as generalities. For example: "People don't like me"; "I'll never be successful." The phrases usually contain words like "always," "never," "nothing," "everything." These phrases and words are not specific. As a result, these generalities creep into all areas of our lives. These inner restrictions keep you from being able to do what's possible. The key to discovering these inner restrictions is to observe them, see what's stopping you, and question it. The first step is to realize that you are inventing these restrictions. The second step is to see where those restrictions might be coming from. Then, look for the specifics of a situation based on the available facts, decide the best real decision to make, and then make it.

Creating Cognitive Dissonance

Embracing and practicing the Philosophy of Possibility can cause cognitive dissonance. This is the sign of growth especially when holding two or more ideas in your mind at once. The internal conflict created by thinking about conflicting or competing ideas, decisions, images, or concepts produces cognitive dissonance. When something comes and interrupts your current model of the world or your paradigm, then you will experience cognitive dissonance.

Be open to the possibility of being wrong.

You may even physically react, feeling discomfort or maybe a headache, or you will feel dizzy when your model of the world is challenged. This is an opportunity to grow and learn, not hide.

Approach and observe these internal opposites with the ability to suspend reality long enough to have a new possibility come in. Be open to the possibility of being wrong. It's freeing not to have all the answers. Others could have a more workable solution or way of looking at something. When you open to possibility, you end up inviting cognitive dissonance inside. The growth leads to acceptance of a new way of thinking and looking at life.

However, when you are resisting, fighting, or are uncomfortable with the experience of cognitive dissonance, you will end up in a worse situation with a close-minded model that you will be stuck in. You will insist on the world being as you see it, not as your opinion or a viewpoint. You will be endlessly and constantly searching for ways to validate, justify, and excuse anything that is irrational about your decision. You allow your discomfort to stop and limit your possibilities and creativity because you desperately are trying to make sense of and find reasons to support anything that conflicts with you.

In the Philosophy of Possibility, I'm a messenger. Please don't shoot the messenger for introducing an open-minded, expansive, and never-ending paradigm in which you are consciously aware, open, and allowing yourself to be wrong, fallible, and make mistakes. This will make a much easier process for you to work from. The Philosophy of Possibility is just another mode of thinking, yet it's an expansive model that allows the absorption of different ideas into your universe. Philosophy of Possibility is all-inclusive and all-encompassing.

Of course, take your ideas from what they are at the moment, and place whatever value you want to place on them. I

> **Philosophy of Possibility is all-inclusive and all-encompassing.**

tread lightly when talking to people about a model that may challenge people's paradigm because it's a great way to lose friends and lose influence on people. I recommend being gentle and kind because most people have everything wrapped around their identities. They are making their life decisions based on those models. When you challenge that, you're challenging thousands and thousands of decisions made based on that model. If they were made wrong about that, then those thousands of decisions that they've made become wrong in some way. Thus, I am very careful about introducing new models into people's thinking. The natural response of people is to defend their paradigm model.

Release Fixed Ideas

Free yourself of the fixed ideas, outcomes, goals, or whatever you think you're trying to obtain. Release them. Let them go. Grant yourself the space to act freely, to do what's necessary. Do it with the hope, or the target of not knowing what's totally possible. This will allow you to accept what happens and quickly adapt. Be fluid in your thinking, while adapting to the situations that present themselves. This is the mindset that can free you from fixed ideas of how things are supposed to happen or be. Often, you won't take any chances because you don't see a clear way to the goal. Every journey starts with one step, and if you have a huge goal, you can't possibly see the goal when you start. Start, start, start; the end almost never can be seen from the start.

Do it with the hope, or the target of not knowing what's totally possible.

Each day, I run eight miles. I actually can't see the destination while I'm running. I take one step after another, and I run up and down hills and past houses and trees, birds and bees, through a golf course. I see planes land and buildings across the long strip, mounted like monuments of financial prosperity. As I run this road that I don't know, I can't see the actual destination of where I'm going. Each time, each day that I run, I get to the destination, and the destination becomes easier and easier as I run it each day. It's easy for me to run the eight miles. For some, that might sound like a lot. For others, it may not sound like much.

Celebrate every step.

You may not be able to see the path to the goals that you seek from where you are. That doesn't mean that you cannot achieve greatness. From where you are, you probably won't be able to see greatness until you start running. Take the first step then another to start the journey. Keep going at a steady pace little by little until you get to at least a first small destination. Once you reach that destination, you can start in another direction to a different destination. On your path, you will meet several people and things that enlighten you. As you get closer to the objective of where you're going, you will accomplish and celebrate many small goals. As my mother would say, "Celebrate every step."

When you reach your destination, people naturally stop learning, reaching, and growing. For example, accomplishing a degree that leads to getting a job. Now that you have a degree, are you done learning? When you realize we've found an answer or destination that you feel or think is good enough, then you stop learning and are limited to this education. We close down any possibility of further learning. We find enormous comfort that there is no reason to look any further.

You may not be able to see the path to the goals that you seek from where you are.

You shouldn't find any comfort when you stop learning. Think about the diseases you had in the past, for which you have cures or vaccinations today. If you had not continued investigating or searching and just assumed that "they are what they are," you wouldn't have the cures that you have today. So when you close your mind down to an answer or a solution, you stop learning. When you look at the world from a standpoint of always investigating and looking openly, you're collecting information that may only be true "in that moment." At any time, the future could change. You act from a flexible position that could

If you stop researching, investigating, and looking around at the market and the competition, you can quickly find customers rerouting their buying pattern.

change when you get new insights in another moment. Otherwise, you would be stuck. In business, if you are not constantly looking, you can become outdated very quickly. If you stop researching, investigating, and looking around at the market and the competition, you can quickly find customers rerouting their buying pattern, and with no income, you will be out of business. Income-Expenses = Net Income or Net Loss. No net income for too long of a period, and there will be no company.

CHAPTER 32

Belief and Knowing

One of the keys of belief is the attachment your identity has to your belief. Your identity wants to be identified with the rightness of your belief. When you see something that appears to be right, you'll identify with that; it becomes part of who you are. When people attack your belief system, you feel like they're attacking you on a personal level. Your beliefs are not who you are. Your belief system is a false identity that wants to be right and avoid being wrong, to dominate and avoid domination, to look good and avoid looking bad. Therefore, distinguish your beliefs; pull them apart though questioning and understand them. You need to recognize that life is created by the beliefs that you have. These beliefs become the lens you look through, and how you see the world.

These beliefs often may not even be what's most workable in the present. For example, early in my business career, I fought **Your beliefs are not who you are.** for the lowest price at all cost. I thought that if I bought low and sold low, I would have more customers. Then I realized that people value quality more than price. I had the cognition that if I live by price in my business, I would die by price. I started searching out products that were more valued by people, that I could offer at a fair price, and provide better service. The result was that I made twice the money and customers were much happier. The price model had become outdated, and if I refused to change my belief, I would not have been in business for more than six months.

You need to realize that what once worked—in business, in relationships, in life—may not necessarily be what works today or in the future. Our belief systems can make us susceptible to a structured environment where our only possibility is a limitation of our options. You need to be openly looking at the different possibilities and questioning "what you don't know you don't know." An everyday person's documentary needs to be done on the anatomy of belief, the deconstruction of belief, the violence that has been based on beliefs, the twisted use of beliefs, and how beliefs currently are used to manipulate others.

Superstition

We love our superstitions. "A black cat is bad luck." The "is" (verb to be) has enormous power, declaring that black cats "are," in fact, bad luck. When you come from a position that black cats bring bad luck with an "is," then you are stuck with the options that are available from that position. Taking this further in life, we have ideas about ourselves—ideas decide that we go into agreements with other people—that are superstitions.

Everything happens for a reason. Is that true? Does everything happen for a reason? Or do we make reasons for everything?

In fact, people get so strongly attached to those superstitions that they bond with others that share this same superstition. A good example that illustrates a superstition—and this is a huge one—is "everything happens for a reason." Is that true?

Does everything happen for a reason? Or do we make reasons for everything? This is not to say that some things couldn't happen for a reason, yet the idea that *everything* in life happens for a reason is a superstition. Becoming attached to superstitions governs the options in your life and shuts down your possibilities. Superstitions are reinforced by the mutual buy-in by other people about how important these superstitions are and what they make up. Is it possible that who you and others think you are is a superstition?

When you uncover those superstitions and recognize them for what they are, you are coming from a place of possibility. A superstition only has power when we accept it as the truth. For example, people can't be trusted; rich people are ___, poor people are_____.

Take a look at phrases or agreements that you've made with many people in social settings that are, in fact, superstitions. These could be all types of phrases from social phrases to cultural phrases to group phrases. You can even get romantic in these superstitions. You romanticize the idea of those superstitions, and they give us a sense of euphoria. That is because superstitions bond us with other people and provide acceptance and approval by using words that we mutually agree to. Mutual superstitions connect us.

Is it possible that who you and others think you are is a superstition?

Our very survival is built around the mutual agreement. There's almost automation about this survival mechanism, which promotes conformity so that you can feel safe in our environment. When we get around someone who continuously disagrees with commonly approved reality, we tend to stay away from them and isolate them from the group. An example is Donald Trump and the Republican party 2015-2016 race. Another example is a baby bird that doesn't act right according to its mother; it risks being thrown out of the nest to its death. When you're with people, you have a sense of predictability that gives you a certain amount of peace. You can see where the attachment to the superstition is embedded in the social culture. For many people, the reality is what they feel or think or physically experience. When they feel it, it's real. If they think it, it's real. When they physically experience it, it's real, even though this may have no necessary attachment to what's real or what's there. You tend to look at things for how you want them to be, how they could be, should be, and would be rather than how they are and what's real. This is, in fact, my personal journey. I am constantly looking and opening myself and standing in the quicksand of reality. I sustain thought and feeling long enough to get different viewpoints to have a better sense of what's real. Reality constantly changes when you look at it from different viewpoints. What's real? How do you know it's real? Does it matter? Why does it matter?

> **I am constantly looking and opening myself and standing in the quicksand of reality.**

What is the purpose of distinguishing superstition from reality? What if I said that who you think or feel you are is a superstition? Maybe that who you are is a superstition. Just consider that as a possibility. You don't have to believe it; just consider the idea that "you" that you think you are, in fact is a superstition. If that's true, then the closer you get to what *is,* and away from superstition, the closer you come to what is and how things are. When you break apart and shatter "you that is a superstition"—or, at least, distinguish that it is a superstition and not necessarily is "true you"—then you will possess more freedom. That freedom is the experience of possibility and has infinite directions.

When you break apart and shatter "you that is a superstition"—or, at least, distinguish that it is a superstition and not necessarily is "true you"—then you will possess more freedom.

Superstition is a realm of options, and when you live in superstitions, you live in the available options that exist to support those superstitions. This requires you to prove what you think or feel is your self-image. One is a mechanism that reduces things down to a set of options that are constrained by fictions that you've bought as reality. The other is a possibility that takes apart those fictions, and opens you up to the infinite potential that you are. That's inherently the difference, and the closer that you can come to accepting that you are a fiction, the better your ability to function and use possibility. Possibility operates from what is, shattering the suppression of your options that are only available from your fictional belief system.

CHAPTER 33

Reflections, Shadows and Creation

Reflection is the act of looking back at a moment in time and pondering on something to get an idea of how to look at the present situation. It is an open area of space allowing you to see the nuances of existence. For example, reflections are wondering, pondering, contemplating, and creating. The shadows in your life are the opposite of your reflections. These are fear-based and constrain and limit you. Shadows are based in fear of the repetition of something that you don't want to happen, and the possibility of it happening shuts you down and confines you. A reflection is a very open space, and a shadow closes you down. When people are reflecting on their past and facing their shadows, they want to generate often a change. When people want to change, they say, "You know, I'm going to change my life," or, "I'm going to change what I'm doing," or, "I am going to change my behavior." They're still attached to the old way of thinking.

A reflection is a very open space, and a shadow closes you down.

You can create and generate your reality on your terms from your space.

When you fight and resist something, you get stuck to it, and it owns you. You have to battle with two fights: the effort to change and the effort to have what you want. Winning in this two-part battle is almost unachievable. You can't obtain that kind of change and make it stick and last. It will drain you.

When somebody says, "I haven't made a lot of money yet. I'm going to change that," their focus is on the fact that they "don't have money" and they're fighting a ghost of the past. The major distinction here would be to generate from a completely new place—what it is that you want and to see that you have it already. "Generate what you want and have it!" Leave your past in the past; it was what it was. Deal with it and accept it as it is. Because the past is unchangeable, even if you think you could change it, you can't. It has already happened!

Generate what you want and have it!Leave your past in the past; it was what it was. Deal with it and accept it as it is. Because the past is unchangeable, even if you think you could change it, you can't. It has already happened.

It isn't about change. It's about creation.

I challenge you to generate whatever you want from a new standpoint, which is that you already have what you want. This way you can create a powerful and unattached stance. You can create and generate your reality on your terms from your space. It's liberating. When you come from there, there will be a sense of gratitude and freedom.

That's the distinction. It isn't about *change*. It's about *creation*.

CHAPTER 34

Vast Content, Lens of Context and

Our Internal Framework

Most people judge others based on the "content" of their life, such as what house they live in, their relationships, and what car they drive. *Content* is everything in your life. It's your past. It's your projected illusion of the future. It's your past pains and experiences. It's all the stuff that makes up your life and has already happened. It is what it is. People make the mistake to believe that their content determines their life and being. That is an illusion because operating from content confines your life.

Context is where you're coming from. Content is where you have been.

Context is a clearer way of being. It's a way of expressing where you're coming from. There are studies that show that we experience about 65,000 independent thoughts a day. About 95 percent of our thoughts are the same or similar thoughts as the ones from the day before. They may be recolored or restructured yet, for the most part, it is the same thought pattern that we had the day before. No wonder most people go through their day almost like being in a trance. If 95 percent of our thoughts have been in our lives for a long time, then our agendas, objectives, and past pains are there to make sure the hurt won't happen again so we can look good and be right. We consciously think about 5 percent of those thoughts. That would be from the "context" of thinking, right? So content is the 95 percent of those reactive thoughts from the past.

Context is where you're coming from. Content is where you have been. You can see a person's "content," like someone who has all that represents what we're supposed to be working towards (car, house, career, wealth) in our concept of a successful person. We think that content will represent that person. Dig in and listen to a "successful person based on the content." Their *beingness* and true context are represented in language. They can have all that "success" and what they express is, "People suck. Everyone's going to steal from you, and my parents have destroyed my childhood. My husband/wife sucks, yet I'm stuck with him/her because it costs too much to get rid of him/her. I'd rather keep him/her than have to pay the price to get rid of him/her, so I pretend to be happy. My kids are screw-ups, yet I'll do the best that I can with them. I don't trust anybody, and I just got to go and get as much as I can from people any way I can, as long as it's legal. Who cares anyway?" That's success?

If you listen closely to people and yourself, we are "confessing," when we speak. Now you can then understand where they are coming from. You will discover what they stand for. What you perceive from content as a perfect life that he/she has, yet his/her context is one that could almost look like hell, right? These fixed ideas and beliefs about life, which is what you operate from to make up the context if you were operating from your belief system, your concepts of what you think should be, and your self-image of what *you* should be. This framework has guided you through life and chooses for you.

You're not choosing anymore. These fixed ideas and guidelines rule you. To go against them can be emotionally upsetting and reactivate past feelings, upsets, and hurts that occurred early in life. We also challenge the survival of our mind, in which the mind's goal is to be right. You make up those analytical distinctions that try to keep you operating, surviving, and making you right and look good, because looking bad could cost you relationships and your content.

When you come from a free space of possibility, your context will generate content.

When you come from a free space of possibility, your context will generate content. From there, if you can look at what's in our context and we can shift that, we pull in the content we get.

Let me give you an example. The word "trust" carries a lot of weight and emotional meaning. There's a certain amount of trust needed for relationships, business, and countries. There are different rules in the context for trust, which run from "I trust you completely like I'm a fool" to "I stopped trusting you because I keep getting hurt" to "I'm not going to trust anyone until they give me complete evidence that shows that they are trustworthy, and they need to earn my trust." Others can be just confused or noncommittal about trust.

All those are based on content from the past. If you're operating from the context and you're "standing from the trust," there's risk there, there's aliveness, yet what can show up can be amazing. Yes, people will make mistakes. Yes, you'll probably discover people that can't be trusted. Either way, you would have experienced that whether you trusted them or didn't trust them, it probably wouldn't have changed the outcome or result.

When you stand in trust from a space of possibility, you open yourself up to being able to have true relationships in your life. If you're in a relationship in which trust doesn't exist, it's unlikely your partner is going to tell you what's really on her/his mind, what she/he is really thinking about, what she/he is really interested in, and she/he probably won't know when she/he is about to leave you. It's when you don't trust, or you don't stand for trust; then people are probably not going to trust you. We have a serious issue.

Talk about trust! For example, you could say to your partner, "I have a concern about trust; can we talk about the level of trust in our relationship?" This is probably a good place to start rather than talking about it from, "I don't trust you, and you don't trust me."

Content would equal "no trust." Context bases trust on the current experience. Only operating from context can free you up.

You could also say, "I have this concern that shows up for me—trust, which is important to me. I want to know that we can experience genuine trust in our relationship. Perhaps I'm misreading it, or maybe it's not true. Help me understand this concern I have about trust in our relationship."

Don't make it that there is a problem. It's not their problem that you don't trust them or that you are having difficulty experiencing trust, yet it may open up a conversation in a direction to accomplish the feeling of trust. Another is, "I had the experience of trust with you, and I saw _____ happen, and from then on, I withheld myself because I was concerned about getting hurt." You come from the space of possibility to open them up, to share what's real for her/him and you, and express the concerns. When you are coming from the "context" of trust, rather than when you come from taking trust from the "content" of life. Content would equal "no trust." Context bases trust on the current experience. Only operating from context can free you up.

Creating Context

This is a unique way of being from the context that you can use the experience to generate the context of your life in the moment. The experience of your context into the world you carve into existence just through words by creating a context of your life. As opposed to a context, operating from your content is operating from your circumstances, things that happened to you, around you, and surrounded by. Stop your content from driving your context. Turn this completely upside down and let your context drive your life and the content will follow. Create your personal context! Steve Job said, "The ones who are crazy enough to think they can change the world are the ones who do."

Context of Influence

Earlier, I mentioned that changing your language and words could change your life and your way of being. The language you use to influence your way of being is relevant because it alters the way people see you and how you show up in the world—your "beingness." Also to that, there's context in which your language brings you into your environment, which becomes the context of your life. The content is everything that is in life—everything around you, every person, car; yes, I mean everything. They're just content. You don't necessarily connect with them.

Context can be shaped. Content is fixed.

What you connect with, however, and what you allow to affect your life determines the context. Context can be shaped. Content is fixed. If you bring into the context people who want to shape your life, whatever it is that you're looking to accomplish like spiritual growth, mental growth, or great conversation, then you can produce what it is that you're looking to produce in your life and get the experience that you're ultimately crafting. That's the ultimate dynamic of creating a life that you want, and it starts with taking control of your language.

If you want to see this in action, look around. People will bring a particular person into their context. For example, they will bring a person who will produce the misery that they're looking to experience, into their context. By doing that, they will indirectly create the exact content that they deny they desire. Whatever you're experiencing, it's because you're bringing that quality into the context of your life. That produces the experience that you get and that experience whether you know it or not is something you desire or feel comfortable with. Some people are comfortable in misery, upset, battles, and frustration, so they'll create a life whether knowingly or unknowingly with the context of which they pull in their life to produce that experience. So you're not really in the dark about what you're producing. You can pretend. You can deny. You can be unaware that you're doing it. Ultimately, if you peel back the onion, you'll find that you're creating the life that you see or have before your eyes within your mind. You're producing the life that you're looking for. Just simply being there can produce an enormous amount of context for your life.

Again, content is everything in your life. Context is what's pulled to the forefront that we take a look at or deal with or experience. We don't experience necessarily everything around us. We interplay with it.

> **You're producing the life that you're looking for.**

CHAPTER 35

Concept versus Experience

When you first meet somebody, and you experience him/her for the first time, you develop a concept of that person. Then you store that concept. From then on, when you meet again that person, you experience him/her as the concept of what you think about him or her. People can be in a relationship with someone who is showing up like a complete jerk who doesn't care about anybody and is inconsiderate. The person you're talking to will insist, "No, that person is considerate, loving, understanding, and supportive." Well, they're living with the concept—believing the words—of something that may have existed when they first experienced that person in the first six months of the relationship. They cling to the concept of who they want to think their partner is rather than who that person "is" now.

They're not in the experience of what they're experiencing.

This can be why people stay in relationships, jobs, and other things that are no longer good for them. He or she got attached to first experiences of reality; now it's only a memory of a concept they hold onto unquestioned. They're not in the experience of what they're experiencing.

It's crucial that you stay away from the past traps, stay present to experience what you're experiencing, be in the now so that you can handle what is. Operating from a position of the idea or concept you have about a person can seem awkward communication between two people from someone who is seeing what really "is." When one experiences anger, fear, and hostility, and so forth, and another person is operating from a previous concept of that individual, they're not going to communicate well because they're not experiencing each other in the present. One has the concept, and another person is actually in the experience while both are trying to communicate their experience. This is often a huge challenge that gets in the way of people's ability to truly communicating with one and another.

When you operate from concepts about people rather than the actual people themselves, you are not experiencing who they are in that moment.

When you operate from concepts about people rather than the actual people themselves, you are not experiencing who they are in that moment. The most powerful stand is to come from what "is" rather than what you hold fixed in the past. See people as they are now. They can just be.

What's the distinction between experience and remembering an experience? When someone focuses on the memory of an experience instead of being in the moment of the current experience, it's almost as if they are preparing for whatever is about to or could happen. They sit there almost like an animal that has been trained, not fully experiencing the moment. It's clouded with memories of past experiences associated with the present experience. They aren't fully engaged in the moment. If they would be more engaged in the moment and true experience, then they could feel fully alive in their experiences.

Take a close look at where you're getting stuck in these associations of memories of experiences. How much capacity do you have to experience in the moment? How much can you take in the moment? How much can you notice in the moment? People get so taken back from past experiences and their concepts of experiences that they miss what's going on in front of them. Many people lose a good 90 percent of their life to this, bringing an experience of something that's no longer there to keep reinforcing their concepts of a whatever good/bad thing, or a good/bad memory of an experience determines the present moment, and they are missing the experience almost completely.

CHAPTER 36

Money Is an Idea

The strange ideas some people have about money includes thinking that there's not enough money to go around. They've fallen into the belief that if one person makes more money, there is someone else who is losing money. They think that if one person is getting ahead, someone else is falling behind as if there were a scarcity of money. Money derives its value on the masses' idea of scarcity and desire for money. This establishes what people will trade for that value. Money is literally only an idea backed in confidence. Our belief in money establishes it.

Money is literally only an idea backed in confidence.

WHAT IF POVERTY WAS JUST SIMPLY BEING STUCK IN A BAD STORY!

Is that viewpoint correct? Is there not enough money? Will someone getting money leave you behind? Does someone who makes money have you make less money? When people get money, do they move ahead of you? Are these conversations real or even true? I'm not asking you to believe me. I'm asking you to take a look. Once you notice what you feel and what you think, you will be able to explore your conversation about money and finally confront that perception.

How much money is there on the planet? The number will blow your mind. There is easily accessible money called "Narrow Money" (world's coins, banknotes, and checking deposits) of $28.6 trillion. How much money can be created on the planet (they're still printing and creating!)? Is money scarce? Total creation through money products is in the quadrillions, products such as stock, real estate, derivatives, contracts, debt, gold etc.

CHAPTER 37

The Secret to Experiencing Love

Can you remember a time when you were with someone for the first time, and you experienced that first blush of love? I mean real love, fresh and new. You had no experience of this person other than the time you were having, and you felt love. This love made life seem perfect. Everything seemed to work. The outlook was exciting, and nothing was unconquerable. Love can conquer all. That is the experience of love. When you're operating in and from your experience, you can truly be powerful.

You can be in the experience of love at any moment!

So what happened? When did things change? How did things change? How do you get the experience of love back? What went wrong? If you fix it, how do you keep it from going wrong again? Why does this always happen to you? You can see other people have the same problem.

What is the experience of love versus the concept of love in relationships? This is the way "IT" identifies your stories as the concept of love. The answer is something you can witness any day or time, anywhere with a three-year-old and a dog: they can teach us to experience. They operate right here and right now, whether sensible or not, reasonable or not. Experience is the most powerful way to love and live life. You can truly hear, feel, see people, and truly be. This is infi-nitely more powerful than operating from concepts. The world is changing moment by moment; concepts devel-oped with the expectation from your identity that may have worked a sec-

You become the living dead when you live in your past concepts

ond ago may not work now. Creating from the moment in ex-perience will put you in the zone where you are and how you are authentically. You can be in the experience of love at any moment!

You start to be in the moment and then down the conceptual spiral of stories you must be right, and just like that, you're gone from the moment. You are experiencing one second, then you go to your past, and you're trapped in your concepts. All this is very safe because you don't have to be in the moment; that would be too real, too vulnerable and too scary. You become the living dead when you live in your past concepts. There are more living dead in the world than people truly living in the moment of their experience. Let us look deep into love from the context of "concept versus experience." When you communicate from the context which is your stand or where you're coming from. Then start to evaluate your content (all your life experiences) to see if it matches the current actions that would inspire "love," you don't mean "I love you." What you mean is based on your concept of love from the past they are demonstrating the pat-terns, expectations or rules for what they think represents love and inspires the statement "I love you."

When you are with your lover, you're hoping that you'll ex-perience love. If your loved one's behavior doesn't match your concept of love, you reject his/her love, and you withhold al-lowing yourself to experience love. This creates distance, the opposite of love which is the expression of experiencing true connection. You hope that your lover's behavior will match your concept of love which at this point can be a moving tar-

When you allow yourself to experience, love fully, it will turn your life back on, and you connect easily.

get for you or your lover and even worse because now you are experiencing disappointment and loss. This is love through the "concept of love"—from rules, guides, and your image of what you think love should be and look like.

This image of love is the concept that gets established in time. Love starts out as an experience of love then devolves into the concepts and memory. These concepts of love track back to what we absorbed as children, saw in movies, heard in songs and saw in other relationships. Sadly, now many long term re-lationships if they are honest will say they don't experience love with their lover very much anymore if at all.

When you allow yourself to experience love fully, it will turn your life back on, and you connect easily. You will feel true ex-citement and enthusiasm; everything will work, and you will be more alive and feel incredible. That's the experience of love. The concept of love is what you fall into and what existed in the past and no longer can be experienced in the present.

CHAPTER 38

Secrets and Mystery Destroy Relationships

When you experience something, there's what event occurred and how you see that event; what your mind produces as associative thoughts that are projected onto and into the event. Since a lot of what you've experienced is held onto like your losses, this pain will be projected onto the current event and create a movie in your minds. That movie produces feelings and those feelings produce an attitude. Then ultimately an action is produced that you take based on what you've interpreted the event to be. Most events are clouded by interpretation instead of experience.

The other route that some positive thinkers take is not to allow themselves to be negative. Instead, they interpret the event in a positive fashion. You can too. Force yourself into a positive action and override your movie. Here, you are acting differently than the way you feel, think, and behave in such a way that you're forcing yourself to behave differently than you feel and think. If it works great, yet if it doesn't, not only do you

> **Most events are clouded by interpretation instead of experience.**

experience the pain you also have the experience of being unauthentic. You wonder if you were authentic would it have worked out. At least you would have been honest with yourself and everyone else from your viewpoint.

Sometimes, it's those events that you see are real, and your thoughts about it are accurate. We as a people are really good at the negative viewpoints. You are not as balanced to objectively looking at it and scripting a story that's positive and without cynicism. This weakness is something that you can work on to become stronger.

See, acknowledge, thank, let go and then decide.

You can see, hear, and feel from an objective viewpoint by letting yourself experience things for what they are and getting in the moment to see it for what it is. When you hear or see those thoughts from the past, just simply acknowledge those thoughts from the past. Hear the thoughts and thank them for being there. Then let them go so that we can refocus back on the current event that you are dealing with. When you have an event that happens, you have neural synapses that fire together, producing all the mental image pictures faster than a split second in our brains to cough up what it is that will help support whatever it is that you're going through. See, acknowledge, thank, let go and then decide.

If you hear something that activates negative thoughts, and the synapses begin the fire, it's fast. An event can fire it off too,

Secrets destroy relationships.

when you evoke this process, it produces that negative mental image pictures of all closely supported past events. You actually may not even know that you pushed a button. And you get this negative thought back, and yet that would be something that really wouldn't bother you in the least any other time. It's like walking around a lion's cage.

In human interaction, you don't know how other people are wired and what's going to create these negative interpretations and associations based on that person's past. Most of the time we're still trying to figure out what will upset ourselves. People think negative thoughts that will have them produce the feelings that ultimately lead them to take the actions that are completely unpredictable and cause disconnection in communication. As a result, people are continuously going back and forth trying desperately to maintain their relationship.

I hear people refer to relationships as work. "We got to work at it." There's this work element to simply being in a relationship. That sense of work in a relationship can be very disheartening because most people inherently are trying to produce actively a positive relationship. They get easily upset because they may misinterpret or interpret something in a way that is negative to them. Even if they don't intend it to be that way. Often they do not communicate their perception to anyone. That hinders further communication because it's hard to communicate over hidden secrets. Secrets destroy relationships. Hiding something can capture our attention and keep us from being able to move forward and connect without first handling these hidden secrets.

This unpredictability and hidden secrets are the keys to inefficiency in corporations. They are the keys to damaged relationships, the keys to divorce, and the keys to suffering in a relationship with other human beings. You'll find people who decide that they're just not good with people. They completely check out of the relationship. They stop relating to others and they stay in their comfort zone to not deal with people because dealing with people can be like dealing with ferocious lions. This ferocious lion in people makes it extremely difficult to deal with their reactions. So we don't relate and communicate anymore because of the ferocious lion that can appear. A few poor interactions can shut people down, and they don't want to deal with further interaction. People sometimes go to covert hostility by developing a fake self that is cynical and sarcastic on the inside and displaying outside a protective layering to let people know, "Back off. If you've got a problem, it's your problem."

People can't find themselves and stop this dwindling spiral of relationships. They cannot develop the keys to being able to have solid relationships with others because they do not have the tools to understand the process to see things for what they are. When you can see things as they are, you will unwind the earlier losses. You will have more predictable behavior because you can spot what's going on and know that it isn't necessarily you; you will be able to manage through the misunderstandings with people to have better flowing present-time communication.

I pursue those special moments when I can look into someone's eyes, and they look into mine, and we experience mutual respect seeing each other having overcome the obstacles towards our objectives and goals—win, lose, or fail. That mutual understanding, vulnerability, trust, and respect that can't be broken or lost. Those are the moments in life that I search for.

Why do we remember so well the moments of invalidation, fear, obstacles, betrayal, backstabbing, and dishonesty? Those resonate in the history of people. The more of those we experience, the more likely we are to believe that this is the way people are. Also, the moments of mutual respect, understanding, trust, and commitment are not as frequently remembered.

To achieve goals, you have to be committed, be all in, be responsible, be depended on, be trusted—which means you must respond to whatever is around you and do what you need to do to have your best interests in your heart. Company policies can't tell you that. The reports that come out will show whether somebody is committed, responsible, dependable, and can be trusted. We are all eventually exposed by the results of the work.

What does it mean to be truly committed, 100 percent committed? What is the experience of that? What does it feel like to let people know that they can 100 percent depend on you? What does that feel like? What is that experience that people can depend on you, yet you don't have to worry about anyone taking advantage of you? And what does it mean, what's the experience from the commitment, responsibility, and dependability to know that you're 100 percent trusted, that someone completely trusts you?

We are all eventually exposed by the results of the work.

These questions are the basic building blocks of human interaction. Everything that does or doesn't flow out of the domain of experience, commitment, responsibility, dependability, and trust will effect and impact every area of our lives.

CHAPTER 39

Experience your Experience and Raise Your EQ

Getting people actually to experience what you're experiencing helps you with your experiential IQ so that you can be present in the moment and be able to absorb the information at hand and make the distinctions of what you're experiencing. Often, just a couple more sentences of listening to somebody will give the experience of what you're experiencing with that individual and be able to make more accurate estimations on what you're experiencing.

For example, let's say Joe, a newly hired HR person. Joe focuses and listens to each person's character, communication, understanding, and adaptability, and Joe displays all the characteristics of a great employee for the position. After being on the job for a while doing routine tasks, however, Joe begins automatically making assumptions about his interviewees. He starts to approximate, hurry, and eventually make bad decisions because he is not in the moment. He is making decisions based on the past, not on the current situation. His EQ of experience was diminished because he was jumping to the decision rather than experiencing the current moment.

In essence, over time, with many experiences, you make

less informed decisions based on these experiences rather than what you're experiencing. If you look inside, you'll see where you automatically go to an assumption or a rule or judgment, when something approximates a memory of an experience. What's difficult is that the memory of the experience is not necessarily the real and complete experience. It's the memory of it. Once experience becomes a memory, it's no longer an experience anymore.

There's no new data that you can get on a memory of an experience; the data that you could get in the moment isn't what you're experiencing. Your memory of that experience has devolved into a concept now, out of which you are now living your life (like the concept of love). That determines how you look at things. Your framework of how you position people and how you judge people becomes automatic. You adopt different assumptions based on this collection of conceptual knowledge. And now your mind is overloaded to be right. Your mind strives to survive by being right and through concepts. Therefore, when you experience from the current moment, from nothing, your mind cannot take that because nothing is death to the mind.

What's difficult is that the memory of the experience is not necessarily the real and complete experience.

What is it that's trying to survive? What concepts are you pushing to survive? This is great for quick adaptation to one environment, yet not for thinking. This mechanism is part of you. It's like your animal mind—the instincts you have in life. When you operate from instinct, you are operating in a very automatic reactive state, reacting to the circumstances in your environment as opposed to thinking, choosing, creating, and generating your experiences through your experiences. So look past your current contextual jar or options that you've created for yourself based on your past.

CHAPTER 40

The Idea of Success and the Experience of Success

I can almost guarantee that when you see someone who looks successful on the outside, chances are they never truly experience success. The "trap of success" is thinking when you get something you "want," that you "need," it is a qualifier to allow yourself the experience of success. You miss the journey, and the journey is the true experience of success. Our society has it backward. So don't miss the amazing journey.

> **True success is a decision with an experience! It needs no evidence to support it with things.**

There are symbols of success all around me—a mansion, race cars, money, influential friends, expensive watches, jewelry, and cool electronics. All these symbols in our society are the evidence or concept of success yet not the experience. People associate the *symbols* of success as *actual* success; "symbol success" that drives people is almost never truly experiences of "actual" success. Actual success is an experience of success. Sometimes that is helping over a prolonged period, creating value for people such that they can have better, richer lives, which end up creating the symbols of success. True success is a decision with an experience! It needs no evidence to support it with things.

Success symbols often come later. Most people are trying to get success without experiencing success. Many people are afraid of success, mostly because they have not allowed themselves to experience what success feels like. You're not told, shown, and don't know how to generate and create success. To have the symbols of success, the best place to start is to create the experience of success such as creating value for you and others—which is the winning of the game of life. Create enough value and the symbols of success will follow if you choose to purchase those symbols of success. So money is just a "symbol" of success. True success is an experiential process. The symbols will arrive usually months or years later than when you made the decisions or acted in a way that attracted the success.

One of the reasons people have a problem experiencing success is that they think circumstances around them will create their experience. They respond to the circumstances around them that don't reflect their image of success. They get in the position **Success happens inside.** where the circumstances outside of them will create the internal success they desire rather than creating success inside themselves in an experiential way, and then the circumstances will show up to support the experience that they have internally that will eventually show up around them. This is a holistic way to experience the "full experience of success" when your inside reflects your outside "experience of success." A symbol of success guarantees you never to experience success. Many "symbols of success" people show to others who don't have what they have to "try" and I mean try because it will never happen. Experiencing success truly does not come from show off symbols. That experience is fleeting.

Success happens inside. Now, that doesn't mean that you

can't land a great job, get massive pay, and save every nickel and dime, and be scared to death to lose all, yet you still cannot experience true success with the symbols of success. Most likely, you'll miss the true experience of success, which can come from "creating value and abundance" over netting of profits. You can call that an override over the cost. You get an override, so you're over the cost of expenses that override margin. You can call it gravy, green mill, or the bottom line. This value you've generated and created over what it cost you. People recognize your value and are willing to go into exchange to give you more than it cost for the value you bring to the equation.

The experience of success is what you're searching for and as you experience that success without mentally savaging. You plant your seeds that will grow into a forest producing fruit for you. Once they've grown into a forest, you'll see people will start to see the success symbols at that point, and they won't see the times when you were planning and planting seeds. They will only remember when you have the plants fully developed and grown. And then they will acknowledge and see it for what it is. This is exactly why for many people the success is so elusive. By the time people acknowledge your success, what got you there isn't there anymore. People get attached to the symbols and forget true, honest journey. People who succeed only through symbols of success and their acquisition, rarely ever and almost never experience true success. That is the "symbol success" trap that spins people in and around infinitely with no end like a dog chasing its tail or like a fish in water that doesn't even know it's in water.

CHAPTER 41

Growth Through Suffering

If I ask you to think about mental and emotional suffering, what comes to your mind? Interesting enough, most human suffering has nothing to do with some part of the body. Maybe for some, it is, yet for the majority of people, it's probably not a body part. What is true mental and emotional suffering? Is it you or is it the mind that has a thought or a self-image that is being questioned, challenged, or affected? Ultimately, this is what's suffering. We create and cause our own mental and emotional suffering by the meaning we give to the events.

The fastest way to remove suffering is taking a look at suffering. How is it suffering? Who are you? Who you really "are" isn't incapable of real suffering. In clearing and releasing each particular idea, reason, justification, excuse, that supports the "meaning" of your pain. This way you can have and isolate each different type of pain that you're experiencing fully.

We create and cause our own mental and emotional suffering by the meaning we give to the events.

Then that alone can release and uplift your reality. These symbols of pain that you have established in your reality threaten to destroy your identity, ego, self-image, or imposed self-image of who you think you are and which you are very proud of. Pride is never a good advisor. You hate when your self-image, self-idea, or self-feeling is questioned, threatened, and challenged. If somebody approaches you with a different feeling, they may challenge the essence of what you think life is supposed to feel like and threatens that very part of your identity.

Take a look at each one of your ideas that you think are causing your suffering. This can and will essentially do the process of clearing that particular pain mechanism. Look and see it for what it is. This is a lifelong process with no place to get to. It's not something that can be one done, you're fixed. The process

Prides never a good advisor.

gets easier and effortless as you go through it one by one and question those things you identify as pain to the point where you identify that your suffering is just an idea. IT is suffering; IT being your mind, your ego. IT is being challenged, attacked, hit. Your self-image is suffering. You, that you who is beautiful, amazing, full of life, and who has the capability for truly living in the moment doesn't suffer at all. You can question, challenge, and eliminate anything that doesn't support where you are going because you are unattached from the anchor that could hold you back. Identities are like an anchor.

CHAPTER 42

Self-Imposed Values and Breaking our Parental Hold

You can liberate yourself from unwanted self-imposed beliefs, values, and constraints. You can allow yourself to have a true, honest choice of your personal values. Imagine taking complete responsibility, having accountability, discovering your truth, owning your natural personal integrity and value, and having no internal conflict.

It's possible that up until now, you've not discovered your true personal integrity. You were born with other people's imposed values. And you have started to recreate and work within those imposed values. You even imposed them upon yourself, hoping that others would fall in the line. You may have even tried imposing through conversation, suggestion, force, or influence the values that you think other people should have. Now is the time to let that go and live in the possibility of allowing yourself to *be* and discover your true personal integrity and your natural values.

Breaking Parental Hold

The process of breaking the hold is breaking away from your mother, father or other authoritarian figures rules that you had to follow whether you agreed or not in your childhood. When we do what we don't want to do as adults, we are outside of our personal integrity. These imagined rules still exist in your life today. To be a free complete adult, you've got to go through the process of freeing yourself from the unknown barriers that are there, sometimes without your knowledge. You may find that when you share your dreams or your ideas with authorities if they don't agree, you can become highly expressed or unexpressed upset. This is a clear indication that they still have, have a hold on you. If they disagree with something you want to do, you get a sense that you're breaking some rule; you're disappointed. In essence, you're "bad." Anything they agree with is "good." Anything they don't agree with is "bad."

"Good" is associated with being in agreement and no conflict. "Bad" is associated with disagreement, and it triggers a feeling or thought of non-survival. Survival of that relationship is built on agreements in most cases. Even if that's an unspoken rule, if you disagree, that is the rebel child that has just the same hold as a regular obedient child because both are reactive in nature. Breaking that hold is a process that will free you of your rebellion and obedient cooperative self-image so that you can be completely responsible for your life. Be the adult who is equal to all people including your parents, grandparents, and other authority figures. It's a process that puts them on an equal footing and the same playing field. Don't worship authorities. Don't invalidate them. Don't go against them. They are completely neutral, equal in nature. Everyone can have their opinion detached from you. Grant them the space to be as they are, completely seeing what they see and simply acknowledge them.

> **Breaking that hold is a process that will free you of your rebellion and obedient cooperative self-image so that you can be completely responsible for your life.**

Create the ability to equalize yourself to your authority figures in your life, avoid being subservient.

Find your place of equality where you can experience or create the experience of being equal to your parents, grandparents, and authorities.

CHAPTER 43

Confessions of the Soul and the Ego

Language is the house of being. Your use of language internally and externally exposes your true being. Listen to people's language and you can hear the confessions of their soul. You can't speak without confessing something. You can't tell somebody a story without confessing what you think or feel. You can't help but confess an idea, viewpoint, disposition, frustration, or understanding when you speak. If you look at your language, you'll see the essence of being, how you're being, what you're being, and to what you're being. Our language is a tattletale on what you think, feel, or experience that you are.

Confession of self and confession of being carve out the ideas, thoughts, feelings, images, and objectives that you're searching for, that are then exposed in your language. Language is what we are talking about when we mention our identity. When you speak of "I" or "me," that it is an identity you believe you are, think you are, feel you are, and that identity is revealed through your words

Happy, fulfilled, successful, and accomplished is a "way of being" in the journey, not the end.

about yourself. That identity will wake you up in the morning and start to project the things that will help that identity survive. Therefore, the language that the identity speaks is not necessarily the one we intend to reveal.

Your projected images, ideas, thoughts, feelings, and mission in life that you have wrapped up in your identity, self-image, and ego are working to feed that unauthentic you. No matter

Remember a lie repeated enough times appears to be true.

what bait is used by ego or identity that you think you are, the "I am" that gets projected is what you need to satisfy for the survival of whatever self-image or self-feeling that you're looking to accomplish. Therefore, your ego and identity will bait you with ideas that once you have this, your experience or survival will be happy, fulfilled, and accomplished. Most of the time, when we get what we think we want, we feel empty. Happy, fulfilled, successful, and accomplished is a "way of being" in the journey, not the end.

Remember a lie repeated enough times appears to be true. True to the point that people defend huge lies, Adolf Hitler said, "If you tell a big

Your language and sayings trap you.

enough lie and tell it frequently enough it will be believed." He took over a country and was on his way to take over the world.

Once you've challenged your identity, it will reinvent itself even "bigger and bolder" because IT is consuming. IT will reinforce the structure of its survival that IT has perfectly designed for your life, and will use your language on you to convince you and accomplish "its" goal. That's your personal cage, jar, paradigm that you're stuck in. Your language and sayings trap you. These sayings have been repeated so many times they have enormous power over you. To get to the truth and answers to your questions, you must escape from the cage that locks you with your words into your jar. The real you lives in limitless possibility and unlimited opportunity. Be impeccable with your language—IT has more power than you can imagine. Listen to what you say, how you say it, and why you say it. You'll be amazed at what you discover.

The real you lives in limitless possibility and unlimited opportunity.

The cage of your language limits your options. You're limited by the cage, which comes from language and what language is using you for. What is language using you for? Your cage has its set of words; language that defines, shapes, and projects what it takes to accomplish the survival of that identity, self-image, or ego. That's a use of language that is pushing you through life and carving the directions. That language is used to manipulate, persuade, identify and support your self-image's survival.

This does not represent the soul, spirit, the actual you and your true self. The language in your ego identified mind is represented through thoughts structure in language, which helps determine what's going on in your universe. But "who" is experiencing your mind, thoughts, feelings, sensations, experiences, and ideas? Who's seeing, feeling, and hearing those thoughts? Your true self is hearing and seeing in a passive state while your ideas, ego, the "I am," "you are" often are taking the structure of that experience and using it. This is putting your true self, soul, spirit in apathy, un-acknowledgment state.

This ability to generate the spirit of who you are is indefinable. There is no *is*; no *are*. It's completely flexible, free, and possible. You can take any shape, form, anything in this essence of you as a spirit, the one that transcends the survival of an ego, idea, self-image, and body. This is bigger than all those limited ideas—each with their flaw because there is no perfect philosophy, no perfect religion, no perfect essence of man, no

perfect self-image, there are no abso-
lutes, only ideas of those things that
we can at times agree upon as a group.

Be without thought, ego or the identity searching to survive.

The spirit is all possibilities. The
self has limited possibilities. You live
within those limits, this cage that is created through language,
and the ego—IT and the *you are*—uses that language to confine
you to the ideas, images, and concepts of your life. Can you instead just *be*? Be without thought, ego or the identity searching
to survive. Can you just be and the experience of what's happening now, in this moment.

CHAPTER 44

Words Are Our Paintbrush

Let's discuss words in a different way than we might be used to. Words are symbols that come together to make a sound. And when we're kids, we mock these sounds, only later associating them with meaning. As adults, however, we're surrounded by newly created words, almost every day. As we use a new word, and we write definitions to define how to use the word in our culture. The definitions often change as people use the new word in different ways. Words change the meaning by use. Words bring up images in communication with other people.

Words are your paintbrush. Words allow you to paint the story of your life. Words reflect the story of your past and create associations with your feelings, mental image pictures, and concepts that you have the experience of in your life. As you move forward in life, pulling from those words, images, and feelings of the past experiences, now concepts, you paint your past into the future. Unless you interrupt your pattern by looking closely at the present ideas, concepts, images, feelings and words that appear when you're in a new situation of now. Words can become like command phrases in your context, and command phrases that have you operating with unquestioned, predefined, prescribed auto responses to a given situation that looks similar to other situations in the same manner.

However, what can happen here is that you're no longer painting into the future of your life; you're painting your past into the present rather than operating and painting from a fresh perspective of *now*. Being consciously aware of these underlying commands and images can help you to be empowered in now. Look at your past, get an idea of the pictures, feelings, thoughts, and command phrases, say thanks for sharing, and then make your decision, yet be present. Often in life, you end up, in many moments, living in a trance.

I use the metaphor of traveling to work every day. I drive about fifteen miles to one of my offices each day over and over and over again. Until one day, I no longer even notice the drive from my house to the office. I find myself in a sense of trance from the house to work to the point where I don't even know how I got there. There could have been several things that have even changed along the way, and I no longer would notice the change because I would be operating from the same place as if it were the same as it had always been.

We operate from the trance and make our decisions from a trance state of living.

Isn't that a fascinating thing about life? That we can get into a trance state with our beliefs, concepts, thoughts, ideas, and feelings so that we no longer are completely in the present moment at all. **The autopilot life!** We operate from the trance and make our decisions from a trance state of living, no longer fully conscious, because we've lived this moment before

The now is uncertain and unsustainable.

because it feels similar to something we've experienced in the past. We are taken out of the moment, thrown into the past, and are making decisions based on the past. You can imagine the hazards of this, and yet most of us, as we get older, get more engaged in this type of trance living. Life seems to pass by at an unbelievable pace and predictability of the same thing occurring each day, to where we fall into our comfort zone—be comfortable, seeking for more comfort, reliability, less chance, less risk, less fear, until we wind up in a state that no longer has any aliveness really associated with it.

Waking yourself up from this trance can be tough. How do you wake up when you think the life you're living is real life? A fish has no idea it is in the water. How do we know we're in a trance? This feels like life. To be truly in the moment, everything we think and feel we are would slip away—so we avoid it. We avoid what truly *is*. Sitting in it can be uncomfortable and unpleasant. Now is uncertain and unsustainable. The past has a sense of certainty for the story that we tell, and the future has an unknown certainty to it. This space of everything is slipping away, it's a battle with your mind, your feelings, with who you think you are from that identity.

If you listen very closely to someone, you can see easily what their true intentions are and what their future will be. Even if they're painting a picture that looks quite beautiful, you can see the intentions are one of destruction expressed in the context of the language and beingness that they are coming from. Their words could be that of anger, frustration, resignation, which you can see and determine the foundation they're building on or creating from. Words are your paintbrush. The palette is whatever you pull from it. If you're pulling from the present moment, the words can truly be painted on the screen of your moment. If you pull from your past, you're pulling from the gallery of pictures that have already been painted for you from the perception of past moments. The possibility is painted on a clean canvas of true creation.

It's difficult to paint a picture of the future if you're painting it from the past. If you're in the moment you are pulling from creativity, the magic of now, love, and purpose. You can be truly inspired by what comes to you in the moment. Paint the picture with your words by pulling in from the space of possibility, allowing new things and ideas to come into your realm. Create what it is that you want to create—allowing yourself to shift off of things that you may be stuck on by letting go, be in the moment and painting with your words.

Word Power

True power is making distinctions, which are what we have been doing together throughout this book. Your words paint pictures. Words can have many different definitions; some words have more than fifteen different definitions! You could use a word in a way that's different from another person's understanding of the definition. So a simple difference in the understanding of the definition of a word can create a difficult time communicating. Two different images and concepts can show up in each person's mind based on the different meaning of the same word. So it's important that we clarify the words for people to develop the concepts in our minds that match up to their concepts to better communicate.

So it's important that we clarify the words for people to develop the concepts in our minds that match up to their concepts to better communicate.

This is one of the biggest obstacles to learning and communicating with people. If we simply clarify every word in the dictionary with every single person that we spoke to, then our conversations would be clear. Therefore, if you hit a block in communication, it may be time to stop and make sure everyone is on the same page in regards to use of particular words.

CHAPTER 45

Deconstructing Identity

To be free and to live in possibility, we must first deconstruct the barriers that keep us from living in possibility. For you to be free, you must deconstruct and free yourself from what you have "become in the world" through the context of our being from the attachment to the self-image and your content.

For you to be free, you must deconstruct and free yourself from what you have "become in the world" through the context of our being from the attachment to the self-image and your content.

For example, when I was born, I had a body and my name was given to the body. This name came with a history already intact, that of the name's origins. I was raised with those elements in place. Over time, other people have referenced the name and used it in different ways and different contexts, from teasing to admiring to a variety of ways. And with each different way, I started to identify the content about that *name* with *me*, with my identity. It's a name that helps people to find my body. It's a name that I'm able to use in varying contexts, which is an identity that I've chosen to keep in existence. The mere existence of that identity and the care of that identity, for example, gives banks a reference point to lend money based on the responsibility that I have undertaken keeping the name and my associated credit number.

That construction of the name, the references, and the numbers that are associated with the name all go towards identifying the body and having the identity that we use in the world. Being able to detach and deconstruct that to the point where you have the freedom and the space to be able to operate, while not identifying yourself with the name you're using, is in the capacity of possibility. Your name is just that: a name. It isn't who you are. And it doesn't necessarily have anything to do with what you are or how people see you. It isn't necessarily anything to do with reality or facts, just simply an alignment of symbols that allow people to find you.

> **So if you're living in possibility, then your name is what makes it possible for people to find you. It's something you use. It isn't something you are.**

The deconstruction and detachment from your name can take some time, and it's never easy. Look at your name and notice how entrenched and committed you are to making your name identity real. In the essence of stating that you are a name, and the challenge with that is if you are a name, you are limited to options of your attachment to your name. Although like we talked about before options are not necessarily a bad thing, they're just not

> **When you realize that you have the freedom and flexibility to enter and be in whatever space or identity that you want to be, you allow possibility in your world.**

space at which full possibility exists. So if you're living in possibility, then your name is what makes it possible for people to find you. It's something you use. It isn't something you are. It's a concept for the ease of being able to make human transactions of communication between people.

This is the essence of being, because, in the realm of possibility, you have a sense of and ability to be completely free. Whatever you decide, you can bring into being by simply allowing yourself and giving yourself space to be whatever it is that you want to generate as being. You can generate any and every identity you want anytime and anywhere. That's the space of the possibility that you're allowing yourself space to become. You allow yourself a sense of freedom from limitations. It's in the ability to open up and look at different ways of being and different identities that you're in the space that can be above or beneath that of which we identify with.

When you realize that you have the freedom and flexibility to enter and be in whatever space or identity that you want to be, you allow possibility in your world. What is possible for you is open, unwritten, and undefined. It isn't historically your past. It isn't even projection of your future. It's that space at which you can be whatever you choose to be in the moment.

Get over Yourself

From the space of truly being without the need for identity, and from absorbing the Philosophy of Possibility, you'll get to the place where you're completely over yourself. You will get over yourself. That's free of and from yourself and free in yourself—"in" meaning a relationship is completely unattached or attached to yourself at your will.

You're not free *of* who you are; you're free *from* who you are—meaning you're above yourself, you can still have fun with your identity, yet it's not so serious. You can make it serious, yet you do so for a purpose, not because you are serious. You can use seriousness to cause an effect, yet you're not affected by being serious about defending it.

That is the point of the Philosophy of Possibility. It's transcending you, your being, and becoming open to seeing possibilities, hearing possibilities, becoming possibilities, and having the ability to let in what's possible for you. Allow a sense of being and thoughts to come in that don't necessarily have to be backed up by your stories, reasons, or justifications of yourself or need to be right from the perspective of your mind. Living in possibility is being above yourself, using the essence of possibility and using every faculty available to allow for the possibility of things that you're not now aware of to enter in your universe and your beingness.

Here's an example to challenge you. Let's say that you believe that John is a good guy, and you've held that belief a long time. Then you witness John doing something different than the model that you've created around John, something that doesn't match up to that belief that John is a good guy, something that puts John in the "bad guy" category.

At this moment, inside your mind, you'll be at a battle between the logic of both of those paradigms, and your neurons will be firing fast and furious on both sides of your brain, going at it rationally, irrationally, emotionally, and raising up all kinds of arguments, thoughts, justifications, excuses, reasons, stories—anything that you can come up with to understand what's going on. You'll be at complete odds with the facts on both sides. You could change your mind about John. Or you could just see a different perspective: that John is neither good nor bad. John is John. John does good things, and John does bad things, from an objective view that John is John. If you hold that to be true, you can see what's there.

> **We have the ability to get into the space of allowing what's there to be there.**

Once you decide and place the judgment of something in

your mind, and enter it in the model, whether it's the left or right hemisphere of the brain, you ultimately condition yourself to be stuck in that idea about that person, which may or may not be true. You'll see what you want to see, and position yourself in the perspective you've created but not what is real. When you can see that John just is, you can truly see John. You can then see yourselves. From that perspective, you can hear yourselves, and other people. You have the ability to get into the space of allowing what's there to be there. And that can be a very difficult place to be at first. To just be there. Be with what is.

Danger of Generalized Global Identification Traps

When you're trying something new, and you have setbacks and obstacles, and you've decided that it no longer makes sense to do it anymore, don't let this become a global event; that is, you generalize the event or obstacle that prevents you from moving forward. Likewise, it's all too easy to do the same thing in other areas of your life, turning a problem into something that is about everything in your entire life. The statement of "the worst things always happen to me" turns into an internal dramatization repeated over and over that consumes you, your life and prevents you from going for what you want.

Free yourself up to experience one moment and event at a time independently of another.

Once you go to that place of universality, it becomes a global trap in which you will get overwhelmed; it can cave you in. The key to staying away from these traps is to dissect the individual problem independently down to the minute, identify exactly what it is you opted out of, and realize that you just failed at that one thing; then you choose to move onto a different path. Because it's *not* a global event, such as, "I never get ahead." It's just one moment and event in time. It's this one event that you're dealing with. It isn't all of you or everything you do.

Be especially careful of the global trap of generalities, because they can overwhelm you. Being nonspecific can lead you to a state of depression. The key is to realize that you are in that trap and start to dig yourself out of the hole by neutralizing and identifying exactly what it is, and break apart those generalizations to specifics and details so that you don't cave yourself in. Free yourself up to experience one moment and event at a time independently of another. This will help you to take the data from that one event and understand it independently of everything else. Your path of transcendence is detaching you from identity, breaking free of your associations to differentiating and choosing in each moment living in now.

CHAPTER 46

Learn to Be Nothing

I have nothing to teach you. I have nothing to offer. Nothing. I want you to be able to understand nothing. Be in nothing. Have nothing, be part of nothing, and truly be in the space of nothing. No time. No space. No future. No past. Probably one of the hardest things to get people to understand is the space of nothing. And it is the most powerful space in the universe. Like a black hole of unimaginable power, and force.

> **Be in nothing. Have nothing, be part of nothing, and truly be in the space of nothing. No time. No space. No future. No past.**

Nothing and Everything

There are two areas where you can excel in possibility. One is nothing. The other is infinite. If you think of it as zero being nothing and infinity being all that is, then you can grasp the two areas. From the space of nothing, all is possible, which is infinite. It's as expansive as the universe from nothing to everything.

Our minds are always looking for a meaning, an explanation to reach a specific position. One, two, three, from here to there—to be able to measure something, that's mind's survival. And other finite spaces like emotions—something that you can feel, and body—the physical sensation. From nothing to infinite is where creation is passed to your mind, body, emotion, and thought.

Nothing and Potential

When you're able to reduce yourself down to the point of nothing, it creates an unbelievable void that allows things to flow into it. That's the space to create when you're looking to create what you don't know that you don't know. When you get to this space and empty everything out to the point where you truly sit comfortably in the space of nothing, then your true ultimate "what's possible" potential can drift into your reality. Allowing yourself to be in the question.

From nothing to infinite is where creation is passed to your mind, body, emotion, and thought.

The idea is that from a space of nothing, all things can come from it because you're not governed by a context or a jar that has to be supported by whatever you bring into that jar. If you let them go and you detach yourself from each one of the different mass jars and contexts you will begin to learn a realm of possibility that will bring you ever closer to the true you.

Allowing yourself to be in the question.

Socratic Method Structure

One way that you can start to expand your knowledge, question authority and increase possibility is through the Socratic Method. This method is one way to discover the truth and what is real. The Socratic Method involves three steps: first is the initial definition of concept; second is to question in a way that brings up exceptions to the concept; and third is the result which is a new definition or way of looking at the concept.

In possibility, we use this method to examine values, beliefs, and interpretations. It is conducted when people begin asking questions to expose the exceptions to their *underlying* values, beliefs, and interpretations to further expanding into the possibility. This will determine that through our interpretations, we can establish beliefs, which can ultimately forge our values. We can also have a value that we establish as a set of beliefs, and then look for the data to interpret in a way that supports those beliefs. The reverse order is valid as well. You can interpret data and forge a belief from it, even though our interpretation is based on a half percent of what's there. This interpretation helps to establish a set of beliefs that create our values. Once those are made, the values seem to drop into our subconscious and activate our paradigm or internal context.

> By digging and examining those, by taking a look at that narrative and examining the possibilities, we can establish a more fluid way to live and give ourselves more possibilities.

Imagine that your beliefs are a pond. When you've uncovering that fixed idea or beliefs and question the validity of the pond, it expands like a river of "the possible you" broadening into the lake and ultimately to an ocean of possibility. From your fixed ideas, you can move into total freedom.

In the Socratic method we will be going into the subconscious or unexamined values that have been formulated to take a look at what we're pulling from—those underlying and established assumptions, beliefs, values and interpretations that guide the direction of our life. By digging and examining those, by taking a look at that narrative and examining the possibilities, we can establish a more fluid way to live and give ourselves more possibilities.

Those underlying values can be productive sources of energy that push you forward. Like an underline drive subconsciously to always produce or work. This is below your conscious knowing of your behavior. By examining your being or behavior, you expose it to your consciousness by looking at your actions and automatic choices. Now uncovered, you can gain control of them by having it exposed as opposed to those automatic subconscious compulsions having, owning, and running you. You can gain control of those compulsions. Even good values that are compulsory that have, own, and run you or are imposed on you by others can create enormous damage when one does not become aware of them in a given situation. For instance, if I were to say during a time of war, "Kill that person, and you save a thousand lives." Now what if you have the value of, "I am not going to kill somebody, ever"? By not killing this one person, you are killing thousands of people, if you stand for the value that "I will not kill anyone." Does your inaction kill a thousand people?

It's a difficult stand in a situation when you put yourself in this uncomfortable position. Your mind is probably now going to lots of places to reconcile this. There are some other means than just simply taking that one life. It will if you're coming from the choice, "I choose not to have my hands bloodied by anybody, and I don't care about the thousand that may die because it hasn't happened yet. I don't want to be responsible for killing somebody for something that may perhaps not happen."

By making that decision—not based on a compulsory value yet actual choice, and the thousand dies—you just made a choice based on an actual inquiry into the possibilities. You then stepped back and made a decision based on that.

What the focus of this book is how you know things, not what you know. What you know is just content. There is an enormous amount of content in the world. Where I am coming from is to operate in a space that is vast enough that your life is based on choice and being completely alive and one of full possibility—one that is not limited to the compulsory options that drive you in an underlying way that you're not aware of, going through life in this sort of trance, reacting to the circumstances that your life presents in front of you.

What I'm talking about is to open yourself up to the possibility, and not be limited to the options of your life. You engage with what you create and what is created. In order to embrace that, be responsible and accountable in a way that's different than the normal terms—not as past tense, yet an active sense— to take a stand and an opportunity to declare to bring things into existence that don't currently exist—generating true creation, and how true creation happens. This process of learning is a process of self-inquiry to find your truth.

You, I, we are the authors of our lives. I don't plan to live in the space of somebody else. I live and have what I have. I grow by growing. I observe what I observe. I experience the thoughts that I experience. I experience the feelings that I have, and I feel my body. These are the messages

What the focus of this book is how you know things, not what you know. What you know is just content.

that are conveyed as a result of the interaction that I experienced with others. And I want to challenge you with questions to explore your life and examine what your underlying values, beliefs, interpretations, and concepts about life are. Through this exploration, you'll make distinctions, discover, realize, and have insights. These insights will give you the ability to empower your life. They will give you true real power.

This word "power" is often misunderstood, so let me clarify and make a distinction between what I see as power and what I experience as true power. True power is influence and inspiration. When I experience someone who has experienced true power with me, they inspire and influence me, helping me adapt the things that I do with the intention of doing something because I want to do it.

Power as the force comes from different places—obligation, guilt, "have to," an entitlement mentality. If I don't do this, then this will happen. That's forced and imposed experience of a "have to"—something that you don't want to truly experience.

Power as the force comes from different places—obligation, guilt, "have to," an entitlement mentality.

Power is something I'm inspired to do, excited to do, and influenced in a way that I thrust myself—into what it is I want to do based on the experience of the person that I'm empowered to be. Force comes from humiliation, disrespect, domination, and control. These are the ways I experience power versus force. So when we explore these questions, it's not to make you wrong, although there will be things that you find out about yourself where you have been wrong. It's not to embarrass you, although, at times, you can experience the thought of embarrassment as a result of going through the process. It's not to make you look bad, although by revealing thoughts and feelings you have about particular things, you could find yourself looking bad. It isn't an effort to dominate you, yet at times, it can feel like the experience of domination, and it's not intended to be.

The fundamental experience is questioning, of truly being in an inquiry—to get what you get, to have what you have, and experience what you're experiencing to the fullest. So that you can get past your IT of options, limitations, the jar and open up yourself to the possibilities to live in the world. The strategy is that you've moving from being compulsory to being actively choosing that, and the only way to do that, unfortunately, is to do the work. Your history will be in question.

Socratic Personal Experience

Your history is in question because this is personal. With this process, the questions are directed at an individual, and they're geared to look at that individual's beliefs, concepts or values—that person's specific orientation with the world.

You won't be looking at it from the perspective of trying to come up with a general answer or get into a debate about the general nature of being or the generalized perspective in which to argue. No. This is personal. By having a dialogue back and forth, our understanding can take flight, illuminating, and creating insights from a deep place—a place of true inquiry, the most vulnerable personal place of your true self.

When questions are asked, look to your experiences, feelings, ideas about the world, and how you've come to know them. That's the essence of the Socratic inquiry into being able to be productive and fluid, moving forward on the track to develop insights. Speak from your experience, not talking about somebody, yet where you're coming from, what you think, what you believe, what you experience, what you feel, what you don't feel, what you don't think, what you don't experience. Those are what you'll be breaking, though. You're not looking for authorities. You're looking for people willing to ask the question and allow the possibilities to arise, illuminate, become, foster, appear, and surrender in whatever ways they are created.

CHAPTER 47

Giving Up Meaning and the Power of Nothingness

When you've opened yourself up to consider all that I've said so far, when you begin to slough off the limits and options to set aside your cage, you may feel a push toward a place of complete nothingness. That there is nothing that you can get or hold onto. It's emptiness. It is all things and everything completely at peace. And it does stop right there. That's an end point, yet not for long.

That's just the starting point from nothing. Pushing *past* that endpoint brings a sense of freedom since you are no longer bound by the meanings, stories, excuses, and justifications of your past or your future. You have complete freedom. You can do whatever you want completely. You have a total sense of freedom, openness to complete possibility. All choices are available to you because you're not shutting them down with beliefs. You're not justifying them away or excusing them away. You just are, and just have.

You may feel a push toward a place of nothingness... It is all things and everything is completely at peace.

You can have anything and everything you want. See the

realm of possibility that is yours, whatever you want to do. The strange thing is most people restrain themselves from this place because not only are we holding ourselves in place based on these stories, reasons, and excuses, but we also try to hold other people to these stoires, reasons, and excuses so that we are interpretred in a way that matches the stories. This stops us from being free and constrains us to our stories.

You aren't meant to live like that. All these things that keep you in a tight little jar, restraining and withholding our reach, containing you that you feel so boxed in and so unalive. Those minimize you and push you to a low level, and at some point, something is going to give. Usually, that would be an end of a friendship or the end of a relationship. That suppression or hold has to blow at some point.

Meaning and Nothingness

I don't think who I am is important. I don't think anybody is of any real importance. We are very much the same—with the similar concerns and problems. If we collectively free ourselves from fear and realize that we can be vulnerable, that could result in honesty and love throughout the world. You are trying to create distance from who you are because when you think you are something, you have to hold up the pretense of the context of whom that person represents and is. That can be dangerous to yourself and others.

Being authentic and honest relieves stress and tension.

Being authentic and honest relieves stress and tension. It relieves you from trying to be something that you're not. That's the essence of "Who am I?" It's breaking the barriers, the context, or rules that have been created by you. Nobody else creates it. Ultimately, you are the one who creates your rules and toolbox for your behavior. Most people are completely unaware that "who they are" is the result of their creation. That it's not necessarily something that is a sequence of circumstances or good fortune or good luck, yet is, in fact, completely self-generated. Circumstances can bump you around a bit, yet ultimately what you generate determines how you respond to and interpret a circumstance.

If you consider something to be against you, then you'll be dominated by it. Let others walk their journeys without taking anything away from them by rules you've set for yourself. Let them be. The nature of who you are is empty and meaningless. I know that can be hard to grasp, yet from that space of nothing, of no meaning, then you have the freedom to create within that space of anything, any meaning you want.

> **Circumstances can bump you around a bit, yet ultimately what you generate determines how you respond to and interpret a circumstance.**

The key is not to be confined. You do the best that you can do, and that's enough to live with dignity, respect, happiness, freedom, love, honesty, and vulnerability. And above all, live authentically.

CHAPTER 48

Question the Model Not the Information

Paradigms and models of the world are quite useful. Let's say, for example, your toilet is clogged. If you know a little bit about toilets, you know that you have water, and you have a pipe. You have another tank that pushes water through, which pushes your waste out the pipe. So you have a pretty good idea about how it works. When that toilet isn't working, you know that you'll see that there is a clog in the pipe, or there is no water in the tank to flush it out. So you either try to unclog it or put water in the tank so that it will flush through.

Not understanding the model would be to see the tank and go over to the light switch and turn the light on, then wonder why it's still clogged. Then you go over, and you take out the trash, and you come back and realize that the toilet is still clogged. Then you wash the car, and you come back, and the toilet is still clogged. In this situation, you don't understand the model of how the toilet works.

Understanding how a model works is important, yet so is understanding the premise. The superior principle of how something works so that you can distinguish what's important from what's not important. For example, if your hair turns gray when you're fifty or sixty-years-old, that's considered common, and you wouldn't go to see a doctor because that's just a normal thing that happens. You may even know why your hair turns gray (loss of pigment in your hair as you age), yet even if you don't, it's normal. If your five-year-old child's hair starts turning gray, that's not normal, and you might take the kid to the doctor to figure out what's going on. There are stable beliefs to reach to understand about senior principles of your paradigm and model.

Understanding the models of how things work is important to our survival. And with most of them, like these two examples, you can physically see and may seem simple and objective. Our internal models, and belief systems are not so simple. They're subjective systems not objectively viewable in the world, yet they are revealed in our actions, which expose them

There are stable beliefs to reach to understand about senior principles of your paradigm and model.

to others and ourselves. The models we hold subjectively in our minds construct beliefs, which rule us, guide us, help us, and hurt us. The only time this can impact our lives in a negative way is when we are unaware and stuck in an unworkable model.

Building a Mental Paradigm

You might wonder how we build our internal paradigm. It's quite interesting, and yet it is organic. Imagine waking up in a dark room, and you walk around, yet you don't know where you are, and you touch a couch. It will be dark, yet you'll have a good idea where the couch might be in the room. You would have a good idea by the positioning of that couch where a TV, a light switch, or a doorway might be.

You start with the familiar and build a concept around it, whether or not it might be correct in reality.

In your mind's eye, you can build a paradigm or a model based on this template and then quickly and efficiently believe you understand the layout of the rest of the room that is completely dark.

This would be an example of building one paradigm in your mind. You start with the familiar and build a concept around it, whether or not it might be correct in reality. You start building beliefs on what you think you know instead of what you really can do.

Shifting Paradigms

When new data comes into a situation around which you've already built a paradigm and that data conflicts with your current model of how you see things, you resist change. This isn't uncommon. You are more reluctant to shift, adjust or change your paradigm. It's more likely you will reject or invalidate the new information. It's because this new information requires thinking.

By judging and failing to shift paradigms, you won't see opportunities.

Living and working in the jar can be very expensive. Here are real life stories on a billion dollar level that today are obviously no brainers: Western Union's board rejecting the telephone from Alexander Graham Bell, Microsoft retaining licensing rights to build PC language and operating system, Xerox's graphic interface that Apple introduced.

Alexander Graham Bell went to Western Union, who in late 19th century dominated the telegraph industry and had a communication industry monopoly. Graham was excited that he could now send voice over wire rather than the Morse code clicks. With Western Union's network, Graham figured since he had the patent on the telephone it was a no brainer. Western Union's board didn't see why people would rather talk and rejected him. In 1879 Western Union left the telephone business, having lost a patent lawsuit with Bell Telephone Company. As the telephone replaced the telegraph, money transfer would become Western Union's primary business.

When IBM needed a language and operating system for their machines, Bill Gates said he had one, which at the time he did not but knew where he could buy one. IBM, proud of their machine and hardware company, saw no value in maintaining the ownership of the Software license. IBM paid for it and gave owner of licensing to Bill Gates, who then launched Microsoft into orbit, making him the richest man in the world.

When Xerox invented the user graphic interface, the mouse and pointer to navigate a screen made it visually easy to use a computer. Steve Jobs heard about it and immediately saw value and visited Xerox getting rights to it. The engineers knew how awesome it was but the board saw no value in it. Steve Jobs got it and launched it in Apple's machines and rocked the personal computer market, which took Apple into orbit.

If I tell you that the San Francisco 49ers and the Yankees were in a game, and the 49ers stepped up to the sixty-yard line and hit a ball out of the park and swished in three points, you would hear that and, knowing that the paradigm of a basketball game, football game, and a baseball game have specific models and specific rules, you would recognize that the data I gave you had conflicts. What would you question? The paradigm you know or the facts as I stated them. We question the data, not the paradigm.

When we know a particular culture or organization paradigm, we can easily interact or engage because we have a model that we understand that works in that environment. We don't have to worry about new data coming in to challenge that paradigm. When we talk about the Philosophy of Possibility, we're introducing new data that will be challenging the paradigm and model of how we look at the world. It is not meant to challenge yet to open us up to more possibilities, and just being open to possibilities will challenge our model or the paradigm to shift, our thinking to shift, our feelings to shift, or our idea of the world will shift.

We question the data, not the paradigm.

That can be threatening because you identify with models and paradigms and derive much of your survival and your mental ability to be *right* that puts you closer to surviving, living, growing, making money, and having successful relationships. The more right you can be, the more you can have. Being wrong is a threat. If you're wrong in society, you're in jail. If you're wrong in a relationship, you don't have a relationship. If you're wrong at the job, you don't have a job. Wrong is identified with all those things, with mistakes that will prevent you from achieving your dreams, while being right means being aligned with the models and the paradigms you believe will bring you what you desire.

Building a Model of Failure

Not achieving your heart's desire can sometimes bring about a paradigm of failure, that you often go into great depressions about, thinking that you are failure. The truth is you haven't failed. Not at all.

The only way that you can truly become a failure is if you *quit altogether*—you haven't proved something yet, or it's yet to be produced. It isn't failure. It's just an event that hasn't taken place yet, and a lot of times

The only way that you can truly become a failure is if you quit altogether—you haven't proved something yet, or it's yet to be produced.

in your mind, you know that you could have produced it, or you could have proven it, and you didn't make the efforts necessary to succeed. Therefore, you develop a feeling of guilt and remorse for something that could have been done that wasn't done, and you experience what you call failure, which perpetuates itself. Honestly, failure is only an illusion. The model is just unproven, underdeveloped, missing something, untested, or unproduced.

CHAPTER 49

Experience Your Experience and Show Up In this Moment

To begin experiencing possibilities, find a place where you can be fully present and fully focused. What does that mean? It means where you are not thinking or feeling about something else. It means not experiencing something other than the room you're in, and the feelings, conversations, and thoughts evoked in the context of that exact moment in time. Get yourself to just "be here." You are nowhere else but here. What that allows you to do is have an unbeliev-able laser-focus on what it is you're try-ing to get accomplished. Most people go around in life with four or five conversations going on in their heads at the same time—a lot of half-finished conversations, projects, and things they need to do that's not complete. They'll be having a conversation with somebody—wait, no. They'll be listening to somebody—wait, no. They'll be hearing somebody while the voices are going on in their heads while they're think-ing about the stuff they need to do, where they need to go. If a part of you is in the past or future, you are not here and now.

> **You are nowhere else but here.**

In many conversations, I have observed people sitting and waiting for the other person to shut up so that they can pretend they acknowledge or heard them so that they can move on to their points. Very few people are listening. They may hear your words, yet they're not listening. This isn't necessarily a bad thing; it's just what we do. We're overwhelmed by content, information, issues, problems, people, things, and life, and it's fast, and it's going faster, and we are missing the experience of being here and now. Are you here yet? How can you get yourself here?

If you're in the moment, you'll start to pull in everything around you. If you're walking through a neighborhood, at that point being in the now, you pull in the plants and the trees, the wind and the clouds, the cars that are parked around and the houses that you are walking by; maybe even the dirt, the squirrels and the

Very few people are listening.

bees, and the butterflies and the sun. You start pulling in the experience, expanded experience of whether the rocks are dry or wet, or if the plants are healthy.

Therefore, the first step of getting yourself to be here is to be fully here. Sounds simple yet try and you'll see it's not easy, yet it can be very uplifting because you can experience the thoughts you have, really experience the feelings you're having and be here powerfully.

Clean Space Breakout

To create that space to break out and break through—to be here—we've got to clean up our words. We've got to clean up

Therefore, the first step of getting yourself to be here is to be fully here

where we're coming from and operate from the space that allows breakthroughs to occur. That involves saying what we mean, and meaning what we say, and letting go of our opinions about ourselves, people, events, things, and situations. We need to focus on ourselves, our experience and clear our minds of the beliefs and limitations that are holding us back. Once we are empty of the past constructions and in a place of freedom and emptiness, we can look at the next steps, breaking through and fill that empty space with the flow of possibilities.

Being with Your Self

It takes a while to clear yourself of old systems of belief, to live in the now, to be yourself operating from your true self in the moment. To just be able to take a walk and experience it as I said above. It's eye-opening

Just experience your experience by exploring, walking, thinking, and feeling whatever is there—let it flow easily out of you.

how much you can see when you're operating from this moment, even if you haven't shed all your baggage yet.

I'm asking you to believe that you can experience what I'm talking about by simply going for a walk by yourself. This personal walk that I am talking about is taken completely by and with yourself. When I get to be with myself, really by myself, I get to take a look at my thoughts, feelings, concerns for the day, and my experiences. I open the memory of the experience of the previous day's events that possibly could still be affecting my life in the moment. It's a walk of possibility—a possibility walk. Just experience your experience by exploring, walking, thinking, and feeling whatever is there—let it flow easily out of you. When I take these walks alone for an hour or more, it allows me to open up, yet at first, though, I didn't notice how much of an impact it was going to make on my business and personal life. If you had said that it would have impacted my life the way it has, I wouldn't have been able to believe you at the time. Until you experience something, you won't know the benefit of it.

When I'm with myself, countless faculties open up for me that don't necessarily open up in front of other people. I notice when I'm in front of other people, I will set a pattern, concepts, or ideas, and I get an approximation of their buttons and what triggers they may have. Likewise, they get an approximation what might set me off. I'll get a sense of what they think or believe or are trying to prove in their life and my strategic alliance in what I'm trying to prove to them and myself. We get caught up in that trap together.

Until you experience something, you won't know the benefit of it.

The freedom to be me is something that I've gotten a lot of benefits from because I don't debate my concepts with somebody else, and see if I can find the right jar. Over a period, any idea will get washed down completely based on group observation and analysis because of the opposing viewpoints, strategies, and games. If anybody challenges, rejects, or doesn't like your ideas, and if you're still attached to that idea, or they are still attached to a different idea, it can become personal. That is how we are rejecting each other without fully understanding each other.

The internal core, the essence of who you are is unobjectionable. Who you are in the arena of possibility is completely intoxicating and inviting, overwhelmingly loving, and untouchable. If the real you were talking to me, you would find it impossible to reject who I am. If I were operating from arrogance or ego or being an identity, then I would say that complete may be objectionable. Yet when I'm operating from the space of "I don't know that I don't know who I am"—from a space of possibility, and that the experience of what I experienced reveals new insights, new understandings, and new cognitions at every moment, and that no moment is the same as the moment before. Coming from here, there is an authentic originality in every moment. Be open to the space of being in it, completely like a child with interest, curiosity, passion, love, and compassion. This space of just openness that's inviting and that allows everyone in and to win and nothing to get in the way. How could that be objectionable?

Identities are destructible.

Develop a vision, to get yourself and people to where they want to get to in their highest self—and not the get too that people develop from the options they think are proving that they're successful, or they look good. Or they're important— things that satisfy the ego, satisfy pride, and a position in the world. I'm not talking about that kind of satisfaction. I'm talking about the satisfaction that comes from being authentic, real, human, loving, free, open, curious, and understanding. Stand for the space that has a vision for you and the world to win.

In essence, the "you" that's not the ego and not the identity that you think you are, is indestructible. Identities are destructible. Names are destructible. Credit scores are destructible. Relationships are destructible. Almost everything is destructible. One thing is indestructible, and that is "the essence of who you are." That space no one can destroy, not even you. Only you truly have the power to cover up and create the illusion of destroying yourself. Only you can buy into a conversation—most likely a historical conversation of something that doesn't necessarily exist in the physical universe anymore—yet if you give it power, then you're live in that illusionary history. You lived in that past moment, the concept of it that is destroying what you're trying to build.

One thing is indestructible, and that is "the essence of who you are."

Honestly, that's trading off

living in past concepts. Now you use some incident, for example, driving under the influence and killing somebody in a car crash, to somehow handle some issue in life that you need to handle. You have forged that moment in time to "keep in place that past concept" to use it for that particular reason now. Having put an effort into grieving and into manipulating yourself with the idea that someday you'll be able to make that okay—that the event at some point in time will somehow manifest itself to be okay—that you'll justify it enough, and you'll punish yourself enough. You'll tell enough people who will say enough things to you so that you can feel like you had some sense of what some religions offer salvation by confessing element of historical events that you're holding onto in the present. Allowing you to let go of it by doing something. How long do you hold on? Why do we hold on?

An unfortunate benefit to all is that you start to use the event to check out of life. It starts to become your scapegoat. It becomes very useful and has the benefit. It becomes a reasonable way not to have the personal relationship you want. It provides a way to explain why you're not winning in life. It becomes an excuse for why you don't engage in relationships. It becomes that side of yourself that you use in that moment in time or that reference piece to explain, justify, and reason with the results that you're getting in life. It becomes the core reason to resign yourself that you're not going to get ahead in life because of this historical event that happened.

Somebody else could interpret such an event in another way and use it in a completely different way because we have the power to interpret something any way we choose. They can interpret that event in a way that drives them to go to church or speak in front of groups to create powerful change. They could tell about this horrific event as a way for people to not drink and drive. They can use this event, in essence, to construct a very different story that can absolve them of this historical event. Be aware that things just happen—what you do with them determines your possibility.

I'm more excited about the constructive conversation to use events to inspire others not to drink and not to drive, over "the poor me victim" story that I have to punish myself for what I have done. If you're still using that past moment, and it's still actively using you, even what you interpret as good and what apparently we see as good, it's nevertheless still using you to some degree. Nothing is anything but what you make it. You make it, and you own it.

Be aware that things just happen—what you do with them determines your possibility.

When you live in possibility, you're in a new moment of time. You actually can choose and say, "You know what, boy, this event happened to me, and it happened. It is a tragedy. It is terrible. I drank. I drove. I killed somebody. And it happened. And now, it's a new day. I'm living in a new day and new possibility. I'm going to share my story in schools and at churches and anywhere. I can be able to express the tragedy in a very uncomfortable way to prevent those events from happening. I will use my horrible event. The horrible event not going to use me. It has worked through my system. It is a past event. It happened. It is. I am going to use it in a way that is interpreted for what looks to me the greatest use of that experience that I can share with other people so that people who are not in my circumstance maybe won't have to experience being the cause of such a tragedy. I'm going to be in the space where I can express that, and I'm going to use that to connect with people—not make excuses—and I'm going to use it to get people to take a look at my experience so they won't have to go through it."

Personally, I have never experienced that kind of tragedy,

yet I had a close friend who did, and I saw the suffering he went through. I think that if you use it in a way that doesn't use you, then there's more power there. You're not defending what you're doing or have to explain why you're doing it, and if someone criticizes you, it's okay. You'll simply say, "I totally understand what you're saying and get where you're coming from." And you can say that without feeling that you have to defend your actions. You'll be operating from a space where you can communicate your experience in a way that isn't defending or justifying the behavior. Simply share the experience.

Be in space and operate from using events rather than events using you. There is power and freedom when you use events, and there is force and weakness when events use you. Those events that use you and cripple your thoughts with never stopping, never ending, never deserving, are the dwindling spiral where you will find yourself trying to gain people's approval, justify your behavior, and count on somebody else to validate you. You are giving your power away to people, things and events and hoping they will give it back to you.

To be in possibility is not looking for justification yet standing vulnerable out there in a space of generating yourself and being you. Stand for you, not for other people, society, strategy, salvation, justification, reason, or excuse for why you're not you. Instead, talk about your personal experiences and how you have experienced successes—results that have occurred out of what you're doing. Do not employ excuses and justifications, which are another way of invalidating the impact of stories that you tell to help minimize the domination that you can be dominated. You don't want to be in a space of domination. Be in your space of power.

You're giving your power away when you start to justify. We all have an enormous amount of power. I've never met anybody that had less power than anyone else. It may be a different kind, or expressed differently, yet not less. I see all people as successful and powerful, who are capable of possibilities that are beyond their imagination, current concepts, and ideas. Look historically and see that it is true, because what we have today is nothing like we could have imagined thirty years ago. So there's the space that is unknown to us. Being more aware of the unknown so you can invite possibility into you.

You give your power away when you justify things, and you provide excuses. You get caught up and stuck and kept from flowing through life. As the result of that, you flow power to something or someone else. For instance, you're flowing your power to the person that you're speaking of trying to justify something. Much of the time you are flowing power to your minds to justify actions. Your mind's objective is to be right about events. You're emotionalizing your actions, "getting stuck in an emotion," yet you deeply know deep inside that they never can be justified. When you're giving away your power to your mind or a person that's receiving the justification, excuses, stories, you and they will feel disempowered. You'll exhaust yourself trying to justify, and they feel a sense of obligation somehow to have to evaluate and judge the event or actions. You've given them the problem, and that's something that they have to reason out in their jar because they didn't experience what you experienced.

How can anyone truly acknowledge a justification that someone is giving from a story of a viewpoint from the past? Both you and they are trying to sell this excuse about something. For instance: what if you're late; no one cares why you're late. Nobody cares about what justifications you have for being late. Nobody cares about the story you have for being late. When they have to listen to your story about why you are late, you're wasting more of their time and yours. In that moment, you're giving your power away, and that other person becomes frustrated because they have to buy into this story they don't care about nor believe. The thing is, you were just late. That's a fact. It was. It's gone. It's history. You're not going to rewrite history through justifications nor explanations. You're not going to rewrite the history with stories. Not at all.

When I started this chapter with ideas about being alone with yourself, I meant that differently than just being alone with your thoughts. That's reorganization and critical thinking and debating the options in your head. Yes, those thoughts are valid. Listen to them. Get through them. Ultimately, I think the more walking you do and time you spend with yourself, you'll get to a space where you can be with yourself, independent of thought, feelings, and body. Your body is just going to do the walking; like a plane on autopilot, and you'll be in the moment fully present.

Experience the world and experience you. Because you, the real you, is undeniable, irresistible, creative, and possible. It is possibility completely discovered. It's the outside influence of being able to get insights and cognitions and information that you didn't necessarily have. You probably find you didn't even know you didn't know that suddenly appears. It's that sense of wondering that might be called intuition or emotional IQ.

I am sure you have experienced remnants of this or an approximation of it. It's that approximating space and having ideas come from possibilities that you don't know you don't know. Have fun from that space. Get the real you to come out and be and generate yourself, which is a playground from what's possible and the possibility that you are.

CHAPTER 50

Becoming What You Desire

Knowing how to become is an art. Look at actors who get paid $25 million to become a character in a movie. Most of the time people look at what they want to become and think, "Well, I don't know how to become that. How will I learn to become that? I have to go to school. I have to get so many degrees. I've got to know the right people. I've got to have money to be that. I've got to do all these things."

Consider the possibility of declaring what you are, and then acting from that stand with conviction. When you say, "I am X," then you inherently start to behave like X. You start to put the pieces together like X, and you're there for X at some point. You'll transcend to being X. So by doing that, you've got to stop fixating yourself on who you think you are. Because who you are is a creation of your mind. You can be whoever you want to be at any given time about anything. You can say you are something, and for that moment you are. The evidence of that truth comes over time, with action and work, and as others embrace the idea that you are X. First, it comes from your declared stand, commitment and conviction to be—a decision that you are who you desire to be.

That's what's so interesting about people who get a job. Once they get a job, people assign them the identity that they are that job. With that identity comes duties, responsibilities, and areas of control. So that person begins to act in the capacity of that identity and assimilate what society thinks about that identity. Those assumptions help them work within a unit of people who identify simply by declaring what they are. How many times have you seen people who are in jobs they don't need to be in, either because they don't fit the responsibility of that job, or they don't have the skill set for it and make rash decisions as a result? Inherently, they aren't that person, even though they still have to assume the identity of that job. It's still not a job until the individual creates the job on their own.

The more you can become responsible for, the more you will have.

That's the thing about being an entrepreneur. You are creating your job. There's no predefined jar, no job description, only guidance from industry magazines, consultants, people in the business, and the limits of legal requirements, etc. For the most part, you're on your own, and you work for yourself. You work by yourself, for yourself.

From this approach you can have as much as you can be responsible for. If you can become responsible for a business, then you can have it. You will be able to maintain it without losing it. Your ability to "have" will be equal to the "how much" you can be responsible for. The more you can become responsible for, the more you will have. Inversely the less that you are responsible for the less you will be able acquire.

I Think, Therefore I Am

*"Two percent of people think, three percent of the people think
they think, and ninety-five percent of the people would rather
die than think."*
—George Bernard Shaw

I ask people to think, which is the origin of opportunity, therefore, I am dangerous to 95 percent of people.

The essence of Descartes's statement, "I think, therefore I am," is in the realm of the Philosophy of Possibility. The disappointment related to this phrase occurs when you think yet you do not become exactly who you are right away. The truth is, however, what you think creates where you're heading and what you'll be. Even if you think you're rich, that will not change the balance in your bank account. I don't care how hard you think; it won't change the amount you have. Those thoughts can determine where you will be in the future. If you think and manifest thoughts like a rich person, then you'll see what it takes to become a rich person. Eventually, your bank account will reflect your thinking, actualized.

What you think *becomes* who you are. It's important to act as if you are that person so that you can manifest and create the thought and actions to be able to do and to have. If you think you're in a successful marriage, and you take the actions needed to have a successful mar-

Eventually, your bank account will reflect your thinking, actualized.

riage, then even if you don't have a successful marriage today, you will have a successful marriage in the future. Make decisions that will lead you to have a successful marriage and have one *today*. You don't need to wait. Everything that represents an unsuccessful marriage is history. It doesn't even exist in this moment. Think it today, act as if your marriage is successful now and watch it becoming successful now and into the future. These are tools and ways of directing your thought and action to have it now.

Be successful from today forward.

Be satisfied from today forward. Be happy now. Be healthy now. Be free now. Love now.

Becoming Bold

"Freedom lies in being Bold"
–Robert Frost

There's a fundamental truth about pushing yourselves out into the world on your own and making a difference: there's an element of fear and excitement in it. Some people, like myself, don't want to push forward because we're afraid that people will disagree with us, or that they will hate us. And that is going to happen. Whatever message you put out into the world, you will attract people who don't like it or don't care about your message. You will also run into people who do care, who write positive stuff, who contribute to your efforts, and who join your crusade.

You will also run into people who do care, who write positive stuff, who contribute to your efforts, and who join your crusade.

There will be the haters. There will be the ones who are made wrong by your right; they'll lash out in whatever way they can to prove you wrong. You cannot back down. You can decide to make a difference and realize the truth of your message, yet also, the truth that you will have people who hate you and people who like you. Both sides are there. Or you can make no difference, no impact. Sit back. Hold your ideas, your concerns, and your beliefs to yourself. Make no difference and create no value in other people's lives by just simply hiding and not being bold because you're afraid. So be bold and express the real you. There will always be haters.

Casting Shadows

What if every loss that you've ever had has cast a shadow over your future? What if what you're looking into and what you're deciding on as far as the direction of your life is deceiving you? These shadows cast a 3-D hologram projection onto your future. A future predetermined by your past that you have no possibility, only options. This is closed to any possibility of the future with no opportunity for something good to happen by your true creation. This shadow will shut down your joyful journey, your brightness, your brilliance, your possibility, the God-given amazement that you are. So cast these shadows aside and keep going into the future, open to meeting the right people, be in the right situation, and to utilize your greatest potential.

Create your future from nothing

Create your future from nothing. Make your perfectly possible future that is full of potential, opportunity, and anything that is possible. Make that future when you can go in front of the people and find opportunities that others missed. Make the future where everything just seems to come together in that perfect moment, in perfect time.

It is almost never as horrible as most people cast their shadows to be.

Living in possibility means enjoying the journey—putting everything, and anything together with unlimited potential while leaving your eyes open to your potential. You must know that when you get that sense of disappointment, it is a cast shadow associated with your past losses that are illustrating the events suggest losing again. You automatically start looking for the worst possible scenario so that you can inherently prepare yourself and protect yourself from what could be a horrible outcome.

It is almost never as horrible as most people cast their shadows to be. Almost never do you ever live in the cast shadow projected onto the future of doom and gloom. Rarely does that ever happen. That shadow keeps playing its terrible movie. You need to be able to pick that movie apart and know that it is only your shadows, yet that it isn't your future, and that isn't real. It's synthetic and only a shadow that you project. You could also project a fantasy of the future that will help balance or combat those shadows to help you live in the moment. You're programmed to project shadows, so it is important that you put out a positive imprint or mental image of the future so that you can, at least, balance your shadows.

Changing Channels

The ability to change channels in being, thinking and doing is crucial to developing. Think of a television as an analogy; you have hundreds of different channels available in your mind as well. For instance, turn on the news channel in your mind; what would this look like? Practice running what a news channel would sound like. Then, turn to comedy and look at what a comedy channel would look, sound and feel like. Turn to a drama and script different events in your life. Then change the channel to a happy channel, where everything is big and exaggerated. Then change the channel to a spiritual channel. Practice each one of these things just by simply changing a channel.

What channel are you on right now?

Often in life, we can get stuck on a channel, and we don't even know that we're stuck on a channel, yet you stay there.

One of the inherent concerns about this is that you don't see the effects of that channel until three months, six months, or nine months from when you were on that channel. What channel are you on right now? What is your favorite channel?

For instance, when you go into a "poor me channel," which is about being a victim and how horrible things are and how life has handed you a raw deal, you stay on this channel long enough and you start to dramatize it and exaggerate it to keep it going. When people have business deals, opportunities, or life events to flow to you, they will not flow those to you. You now have the energy of somebody who is in a poor me channel that doesn't match flowing life or business to you. You're going to attract the energy that supports the poor me channel. How much action happens in that channel? So if you want to limit the opportunities that you have, start a poor me channel. If you want to do an action-adventure, turn into an action adventure channel, and you'll attract people who are into action and adventure.

Can you change your channel?

Can you change your channel? Changing the channel and shifting in the moment is a huge power you can possess so that you can quickly get off a channel and onto the channel that is going to work for you. Choose and create your channels!!

CHAPTER 51

Break Away from Decisions Based on Deductive Reasoning

Living with your current options in your jar, is similar to making choices based on deductive reasoning—you deduce what you're doing now, so you break it down and make decisions by reducing your options. With this reasoning, you're heading more and more towards a concentrated finite answer that you're looking for.

> So possibility thinking is really about expansive reasoning, not deductive reasoning.

This is not reasoning from possibility. The possibility is not reducing what you're trying to accomplish onto one finite justified decision. When it comes to making a decision, deductive reasoning can be extremely important and vital to making decisions. In the area of creation, possibility thinking allows you to explore new possibilities, to expand your options and heads you in the direction of infinite understanding and possibilities—into that part of the mind that allows for creativity and imagination to spawn outward rather than inward. So you go in the direction of expansion as your process. You expand your possibilities into the space of where you don't know what you don't know, which is where possibility thinking comes into play. So possibility thinking is really about expansive reasoning, not deductive reasoning.

As you start to learn what you don't know, it expands space even further—if you think of that space as a sphere, there's a point that is everything you know. Now everything you know touches on another space, which is what you don't know. Now what you don't know you don't know is actually what touches on the outer perimeter

Leap into the space of uncertainty that is beyond your observation.

of what you do know you don't know, and the space that we're speaking about is expanding what you don't know and reaching farther out in what you don't know you don't know—that uncertain space, the same space that's communicated in the idea of quantum physics.

Physics is in the realm of what we observe and understand rather than things that we see and observe yet don't understand. Leap into the space of uncertainty that is beyond your observation. Because to know or not know is to know with certainty that you don't know that you don't know. That space of uncertainty; this is the realm and space of possibility, that which you don't know you don't know.

The lower you are mentally, spiritually, and emotionally, the more circumstances will influence your life.

To evoke that, we have to open up space and look past our guides, rules, or laws of thinking and go beyond them and prepare to be surprised.

Circumstance and Consciousness Evolution

The concept or construct of life is when your circumstances and your spirituality or your consciousness meet. Consciousness versus circumstances—which is more in control? The more highly evolved you are spiritual, intellectually, and physically, the more you're able to influence your circumstances. The lower you are mentally, spiritually, and emotionally, the more

"To hell with circumstances; I create opportunities."

circumstances will influence your life. Both exist cohesively at the same time. Your ability to move your circumstances in the direction that you want them to go in is influenced by your level of development, so the key to overcoming circumstances is to focus on the evolution of your intellectual, spiritual, and emotional well-being.

You'll also be strong if all three facets of your life have equally strong development. Your spirit is your overall "database." The stronger and more evolved the consciousness of your spirit; you will possess higher intellectual and emotional capacity. Like buttons on a communication terminal, the more lights that come on, the more things that you are aware of, the more evolved you are. As your awareness level grows up, your spirit can communicate intellectually through those lights that have come on through the evolutionary process of cognitive thinking. Turn on the lights and connect the dots. The more dots you connect, the wiser you can be and the more you're able to influence situations. As Bruce Lee once said: "To hell with circumstances; I create opportunities."

On Peace during the Evolution of Awareness

There's a period in the evolution of your strengths growing out of your jar when you will be working for your identity, or identity will be working for you. It will involve a daily struggle separating these two. Then as you evolve, you'll start to work in those identities by checking and evaluating them out, moving them around, managing and playing with them. You're managing your identity, your purpose, and your idea. Then as you progress, you'll start to work on those, the "who" you are and what you could be. You start to shape that which is you rather than being trapped in you.

You start to shape that which is you rather than being trapped in you.

This progresses into a sense of peace that you will have when you become whatever it is you choose to be. You will grow in any direction you choose. All possibilities will be open to you. You will be completely free and at peace with your environment and the things in your life. You will accept things, not like surrendering as they are, not as the way you want them to be, that would be arguing with reality. The way you want things to be is not true now. Now you can effectively change them. If you're still arguing with the past that is unchangeable, it's ineffective. You might be able to rephrase the past, so it is more palatable, yet ultimately it is what it is.

This is the difference of the evolution from your identity having you to you really having it, to working in it, to working on it, to being self-aware of it completely. Where you have that awareness and peace to be able to manipulate and do whatever you want. You can change it, evolve it, give it up, make it so—create it. You have the complete, real and true ability to live in this flexibility reality.

CHAPTER 52

Creating the Space for Possibility

Creating space is probably a pretty foreign concept for most people—the idea of being able to create space. I want you to look inside yourself. How much space is there for you to operate in? Do you experience a sense of confinement to a set of options, a set of rules, a set of governances? Your name has a set of rules, attachments, and things that are associated with it— the name your parents gave your body, where you're from, who you are, and what set of options and rules you operate from. It doesn't allow you to create much space. When you look at other people, you look from the space of judgment and criticism, the space of trying to get to who they are, who they are, or why they do what they do. How much space do you give others?

You can create space. The more you identify with someone, the less space you give him or her. Open yourself to the possibility of who you are and the possibility of who others are and who they can be. I'm open to the possibility of you—who you may become and who you might have been. I'm open to you. I'm creating space—not for whom you have been or are yet, but for what's possible for you.

How much space do you give others?

I'm operating from the space that there is a possibility of you. Allowing my thoughts to "be in the question of you." So I can see who is really there in the moment. From here we open up space, giving people space, so they can be in the moment and express themselves, and they can be received in this space. Because you have a relationship, you're relating. The relationship isn't a thing. It's the relating that goes back and forth—space, whereas people can relate in space.

When you're relating in the space of possibility, you're opening up the person to the idea that they are possible. When you're looking at the possibility of others and of "I am," you enter space and the ability to relate back and forth. When you operate from beliefs and concepts about people from criticism and judgment point of view—from a fixed idea about who a person is—your brain will look in this conversation to be right and support those ideas and keep those ideas surviving. We classify people. We have to discover their character because that's who they are. When people change, we heavily question that. Is that who they are? You'll have a hard time accepting something different other than your decisions about them.

You are powerful in the space of possible granting people and yourself space to BE.

When you look at people from your space of possibility, you give them the space to accept what is possible now. From that space, miracles can be created. It opens doors. It opens eyes. It opens ears. It opens up the relationship of what could be. That's the space of possibility of what's possible. You are possible. I'm possible. We are possible. You are powerful in the space of possible granting people and yourself space to BE.

"I Am Being" Exercise

Take a few minutes to try an exercise to get you started. Find a place to sit down where you won't be disturbed. Sit there and be with yourself. Be. Work to be there with no thought, no feeling, and no experience. Truly be.

Often, in the moment, a thought will come up in your mind as an exercise to see what is justifying its beingness, to explain why it's there, to remember the reasons that we brought up the story and what it represents. See it and do nothing with it; let it flow. Allow it to go without justifying it being there, without reason, without any story or explanation why it showed up. Allow the thought that comes up for you without doing anything. See it. Let it go. Sit there and be with it until it fades. See the next thought of you just being without a thought, without any explanation, without any story. See your thoughts pass and experience the experience without the analyzer of your mind. You must experience an experience with no need to interact with your analyzer. Let go as it fades. Whatever impression, thoughts, stories, reasons, or justifications you might have about it, both in support of it and against it, allow those to be, let them come in and flow out.

Be in this moment. Experience this moment.

Be in this moment. Experience this moment. When you find that you're there, part of this exercise is to notice what it is to "be." When you're being, you have the ability to adapt to any situation and find out what you need to do without bringing in something to cloud and cover up the judgment or acting on an impulse. Also, you'll notice that when something comes up, and you're doing something contrary, look where you go back into yourself to come up with excuses. Experience when you're coming up with those excuses and justifications to rationalize that which is, not just having it be what it is. We have to explain, justify, reason with it, or have a story to it, the necessity for you to carve meaning into every moment of your life and the purpose for that—the justification, excuses, and stories for being. That is, in essence, weakening who you are.

When you come from the state, "I am powerful. I am courageous." what comes up for you? When you look at something, and you say, "I am powerful." Then you have it. You don't have to justify, explain, and prove. When you go back, and you look at something, and you're trying to figure it out—perhaps a moment in time in the past, where you weren't feeling courageous, comes into play that can keep you from being courageous in the future. These things cut your reach, your power, your courageousness, your risk, and your ability to be. The process here is about being able to say, "I am." The "I am" that is completely individualized from any other moment or experience. Then whatever it is you are, whatever would be necessary to get where you want to go or do, you allow that to be. Let everything that stops you dissipate so that they're not in your way or not pushing you to justify that you are something, that you can do, be, and have whatever you want in life.

CHAPTER 53

What Comes First, Emotion or Thought?

I am a theater and film actor. I qualified for the film actors' union, the Screen Actors Guild, after getting a part in a movie with Robin Williams, *What Dreams May Come*, where I played a warrior in hell, yet my part with Robin was cut out. That's life. One year, I did several films and theater qualifying for the theater union, the Actors Equity Guild. While in training as an actor, I would sometimes take on the physical characteristic of a role and the emotion and thought would follow. Other times, I would focus on a thought and repeat it over and over until I could feel the emotion and my body would change the position to support the emotion. Other times, I could jump right into feeling an emotion and my body would follow. I love acting. It is so much fun when it all comes together and looks completely real, and people can feel you.

There is neuroscience that supports this method. It demonstrates the neurochemistry that happens in your mind. Sit in a room by yourself and yell anything at the top of your lungs. Then note the thoughts you have about that. Repeat this exercise; do it several times. Notice how your thought patterns start to change; this reflects how the chemistry in your brain is changing. Then watch a deep love story, and then note the chemical changes that occur after watching it. This exercise simply shows that you can activate your neurochemistry system at will. By activating this internal system in the thymus chemical cocktails are mixed and create the chemicals that will send neuro-

Emotion affects thoughts.
Thoughts affect emotions.

peptides through the blood stream to dock in every cell in your body and to give direction to stimulate the neural synapses to fire in the areas that produce the thoughts based on the area you're demonstrating. So what you're using is your emotion to create your thoughts.

By doing an action that creates a specific emotion, you stimulate your neurons—your neural synapses—so that your neurons will start firing together in a specific order. Those orders are connected to the consciousness and thoughts that are in the arena that brings back your past incidents and what you'll think about in that moment. So I'm using a backward exercise to show this process of creating an emotion to trigger thought. Emotion affects thought.

Thoughts affect emotions. Hold a thought of someone you feel for very deeply. Repeat the thought and romanticize the thought repeating it over and over until you experience activating many of your neurons. Neurons in a specific area, firing specific thoughts that stimulate the thymus to be able to create the chemical cocktail to be able to make specific neuroreceptors, receive the specific chemicals that signal the thymus to create the chemical cocktail that will send out neuropeptides in the blood stream to dock to the cells in your whole body. In essence, what you're doing here is to use your thought pattern to dope your body with specific chemicals to create emotion. You create all your emotions! So you can have an emotion that you create through action that can create the thoughts or you can have the thoughts that create the emotion as well. Then you can also have some simultaneous combination of both at the same time. Like a triangle connecting your physical action, you can use thought and emotion in any order to influence the other two.

Your subconscious can trigger emotions that act below your awareness first, and then your thoughts will precede those and can create the emotions. It can be very subtle. Ultimately, you want to do these exercises to raise your awareness to the idea that if you feel bad, it's not necessarily you feeling bad. Your thoughts are producing chemicals that produce the emotion that creates addition thoughts strengthening this cycle. Interrupt the cycle. Over time, the subconscious—the "IT" will have less and less automated influence over you. Your thought, feelings, and life will not be a subject, so that is so unpredictable and random.

You might sometimes feel that you are your emotions or think you are your thoughts, depending on what you identify most with.

You might sometimes feel that you are your emotions or think you are your thoughts, depending on what you identify most with. What dictated your experience thought/emotion? What experience do you feel you're not responsible for or have power over your thought/emotion? The essence these forces can force you to feel or think that you're actively not responsible for the emotions and thoughts that you have. This awareness that you own your thoughts and emotions, and not them owing you, will raise you up from being in the life of circumstances to a life of being at "cause." From being kicked around by life yet being aware of your internal process and how it affects what you do and think, your relationship with life, yourself, and with people around you, so that you can create whatever it is that you want to create now.

The Effects of Your Mind, Body, and Emotions

Your mind, your body and your emotions have distinct effects on yourself. It's that part of you that's able to witness emotions, thoughts, and your body's experience. To give you an example of how the body plays on emotions, when your body's survival is threatened, the vibration in the cells of your body drops to a level that brings your emotional vibrational tone down. If your body's survival is threatened, you will get to the vibrational point of fear. If you're tight and rigid physically, the vibration you're going to feel is angry. If you don't eat, your energy level and your emotional vibration level will drop, and your thought process will be influenced. Ultimately, the survival of your body reduces to the survival of your frequency or your emotion within that body. Then your thoughts get drawn in. They interplay with each other.

One can dominate others, and often a strong thinker can influence emotion and ultimately his or her body. An emotional person can influence their mind to a large degree as well as their body. If you're angry all the time, your body's system produces neuropeptides from your thymus that go into your system and hit your cells and will dope them constantly, almost like drug abuse. Just like anger in your external life creates damage with people, you can have cell damage created by being constantly angry. Anger can cause heart attacks and strokes. Many people get addicted to the drug of anger or sadness.

> **Ultimately, the survival of your body reduces to the survival of your frequency or your emotion within that body.**

People who work out a lot using their body, or eat a lot using their body, can dope themselves up. You can eat a lot of products that make you feel good. You're using your body's system to influence your emotions, which ultimately influences your mind and happiness. These are components that are all within reach of handling.

The whole idea is being aware and empowered, realizing that you can handle each one of these things to navigate life and create more in the world. You could give more services, products, ideas, and make a bigger difference in people's lives. Because the better you can handle your physical, emotional, and thought self, the faster and more productive you are. Trust me, if you have depression, you lose a lot of production in the process. You might think it unbelievable when you're in overt hostility, and you're angry, and you're pushing, yet ultimately, that's not necessarily going be your highest possible self.

In essence, the idea is to do exercises that show when you're in an emotion what thoughts come to mind and how you feel emotional and how your body feels. Your emotion is something that is like the color on a canvas. What is your physical body's experience now? What is your emotional experience now? What are you thinking right now? Be aware and be a cause.

Positive and Negative Thoughts

We have positive thoughts and negative thoughts. When you have constructive thoughts about doing something, and then you get counter-constructive thoughts, you balance out to a neutral state, which typically results in doing nothing. For example, you may start out thinking that landscaping would be a great business, and have all positive thoughts and get started. Then you realize that counter-productive thoughts have developed, and it can neutralize your business to the point where you were no longer successful because you are discovering all things you wouldn't like. So your positive thoughts neutralized by your negative thoughts create a sense of staleness or a stop.

To be successful, as those negative things come in, it's necessary to process them and then create new powerful positive thoughts that empower you. Empower you in the direction of your ultimate goal, so that those counter-thoughts that come at you are handled and now you are more aware of your goal that pushes you forward.

If you walk around life positively charged, there's a very good chance that the negative people will be pulled in to neutralize your positivity. If you're negative all the time, you'll pull in positive people who are looking to neutralize your negativity, a lot of times from a position of help. Going in a neutral state into a situation allows whatever is there to resonate with that neutral state so that you're not coming into it positively charged, where you end up in a devil's advocate conversation, or negatively charged, where you can end up being shut down.

To be successful, as those negative things come in, it's necessary to process them and then create new powerful positive thoughts that empower you.

CHAPTER 54

Free Yourself of Obligation, Guilt and Duty

Obligation, guilt, and duty don't exist in the Philosophy of Possibility. Why not? Because those words confine you to the responsibility of an option rather than recognizing that you have free will. Options thinking is doing something out of the obligation, duty, guilt. You hear many times: "If I don't do this, then this will happen." Guilt is a mechanism of anger directed at you to change. If you're angry enough with yourself to change from guilt, then you want to do it in the first place; you're fighting against yourself foolishly. Duty implies that you don't necessarily want to do it, right?

The possibility is openly reaching beyond duty, obligation, and guilt. The possibility is turning each of those into a joy, opening it up to what's possible. Explore getting more out of that moment than just "have to" which is the key to discovering you are operating from duty, obligation and guilt. Turn that into a "get to": you get to live, you get to do. You get access to people that are in your life, and if you want to call that duty, obligation, and guilt, then you're living in

> **Guilt is a mechanism of anger directed at you to change.**

the options, and the truth is you don't have to do anything. So stop lying to yourself that you have to do something. It's a get to, and you're only playing yourself, not anyone else. You spread that negative goo around on people, and you push them away and confine yourself to options.

As a child, I would see my biological father every other weekend, and I could tell that I was an obligation, guilt, and duty to him. My stepfather, on the other hand, showed up to every soccer game and every event that I did and was excited to be there. It wasn't like he had to be there; he wanted to be there and be a part of my event. My stepfather seemed to be connected to me; he felt every event I was in. He wanted to see me win in life. He wanted to see me grow. He pushed me beyond the limits that I thought were possible. He'd always question me when I thought I couldn't do something, whether that was true or my imposed limitation. He pushed the possibility that anything that I wanted to do was possible. I found myself letting go and going with it. I dare you to let go and go with your possibility.

So stop lying to yourself that you have to do something.

I dare you to let go and go with your possibility.

It was the same with my mother. She did the same thing. But when I went to my biological father's house, where I felt like an obligation, my stepmother seemed to dislike me and constantly criticized almost everything I did. Her body language was expressing that I completely annoyed her. There was no language about being proud or anything that had to do with growing me as a person. There was this sense of what not to do.

Conquer Time

What is your relationship with time? What is time for you? If I could help you or assist you with time, what would that look like? Would you want to have more time? Would you want to spend more time with the people you care about in your life? What is a time in your past? What does your future look like relative to time? Time is different for the individual, yet there's a personal relationship with time and for many of us, that relationship is probably not a very good one.

Normally, I'm up at 5:00 am, yet if I don't get up until 7:13, I immediately have a negative feeling, a feeling of anger that comes into my body. Then I have the associative thoughts related to anger, and that starts to fire off the thoughts that bring me down. Then, I think about each thought, about what I will not get done as a result of sleeping two more hours, and I start to regret waking up at all—in this sense, anger that turned to regret.

What I noticed from this is that I don't have time. The time has me. I'm not operating with the use, power, and control of time. Time is using me. The concept of time that I have has outmaneuvered me in that moment; my thoughts are at work against me in that moment. So before I've even gotten out of bed, I'm experiencing time in a very negative way, feeling angry about it and having thoughts about it that are starting out my day against. Before I've even started my day, I was thinking of the day before and all the things that I wanted to get accomplished that didn't get done.

I was doing a $12 million project, and values of real estate were going up month after month. I saw the opportunity to delay the project as long as I could because values were going up. In September 2008, the values had drastically dropped, and my bank failed. The project still had a million dollars left to complete, and I wasn't able to complete it because I was operating from a credit line and didn't have to make payments on the loan yet. The payments to the loan were already in the credit line plus the interest reserves. The bank pulled the advanced payments and interest reserves from my account. In development, you only get paid for the money that's dispersed from the project, not the full loan, until you've drawn all the money out.

Here I am delaying it because I want to disperse as little as possible so that I'm using as little as possible for the payments and interest, and then my bank fails. Two and a half years later, the project sold to an investment firm that approached me. I said we have a million left to draw on the credit line and finish the project to sell. They saw an opportunity to make twice as much. They did not advance per the contract and foreclose on the property and still went after me for the loan amount of $4.8 million. My biggest stain about time is the stain of this project.

When I noticed the time at 7:13 in the morning, I started looking at the thoughts that were being generated by this negative experience of time. Now that event no longer exists. It is gone, and yet, it persists in my mind as if it were a current-day consequence to not getting up out of bed, which is a negative driver. What you might think would be positive impact to get more done is a negative driver, and that negative driver will be the "come–from" to produce the results in my day, which is not an empowering one. It's a "come from" that will produce weakness, and I'm operating my day from the force rather than power. This force will have me make decisions that aren't necessarily the best decisions for what I'd like to accomplish in a day because I'm coming from the force, not power. This force will have me make decisions, operate, and come from a sense of fear, anger, frustration, and a lack of hope.

I'm not being in the moment of time. I'm operating from a concept from the past and reliving it each day in the moment almost like hell. Yet unexamined, without looking at it deeper, I wouldn't be able to expose it for what it is and see what I'm operating from, unless I take a look at the first thought—what I didn't get accomplished the day before—and then the thought that comes from that thought which leads to the thought of not being able to accomplish that goal, and then the string of thoughts that accompany it. Uncovering those and looking at them and being able to let them go is the power that lies in being able to operate from time to regain that sense of time in the moment, looking for that space to operate from the ability to have time.

I know it sounds like a semantic argument, and it probably may not seem like very much, maybe even overly analytical in the moment. Look at it in the space that I'm talking about, where time has you, and you don't have time. If you're operating from a concept, you're operating from the past or an image of the future. If you operate from the presence of time and being in the time as it is, where it is, how it is, and having it, then your conversation about what you could have, would have, should have, might have wanted to do that occupies a tremendous amount of time in

Let go of the conversation of what you don't have, a scarcity concept, or what you could have. This distances ourselves from the present moment.

our everyday existence—this existence of not being present. I'm not talking about the space of being here now or the power of now. You have what you have and what has already happened.

Let go of the conversation of what you don't have, a scarcity concept, or what you could have. This distances yourselves from the present moment. The present moment is what you're operating from, and in that moment is what you can do anything about anything. You can't do anything about your past. Your past is a myth of what you think was, and that myth has lots of viewpoints. If you ask a hundred people, you'll get a hundred different viewpoints of that event—literally one hundred images of what happened.

People project their agenda onto the moment. Since most people are not fully present, they take whatever they were thinking about in the moment, such as what they could have or should have, and it's mixed like a stew with the current moment. They bring their experience of the past to the current moment. So it's no longer the current moment. It's the moment mixed with past experiences, trying to be right about that past.

The complex mental twists that people will make to have a current moment to be somebody who reflects an experience from the past and a fear projected into the future. These mental gymnastics are so they can be right about the experience they had. Also, they often seek a justification for why they don't have to do what they want to do or what you want them to do or what needs to be done. This moment of time, mixed in with the past, mixed in with the future fears or possibilities, obstructs the viewpoint. Therefore, when you have a hundred observers observing one moment, you're going to get a hundred different observations of that moment, much like the telephone game you played in school. As the whispered story circulates, it changes until the outcome is completely different from the original based on a story and each person's agenda, an event will result in a different a story when it communicates from one mouth to the next.

It's the moment mixed with past experiences, trying to be right about that past.

People hear what they want to hear. They see what they want to see. They experience what they want to experience. That's the romance of getting to be right about that moment. What we're looking for in the moment is to be completely present, or as much as you possibly can, to be like a muscle that you exercise to see what's there, look at the current moment, and keep looking at it. Hold yourself there, open yourself up to more possibilities, allow your automatic thoughts to pop out and look at them as a commentator or a reporter. To hold that place so that the thoughts don't have you and you can look at what's there. You can be completely present in the moment, past your thoughts, feelings, concepts, ideas, and images about what it should be and see it for what it is in the moment. From that cleared space, you can truly have time. It won't have you.

You have time conquered when you use time and time doesn't use you. People who look to lead can multiply their time by engaging and empowering people towards an activity, and by providing value in the society that creates enough production to support their efforts. In the common agreement, this value comes from the people who are doing the production, the management which has empowered them, and the customers who ultimately keep them surviving and thriving.

You can conquer time, yet first, you have to confront it and confront your relationship with time, confront your thoughts, concepts, images you have about time, and confront time completely. Be with it and accept time, not as a resignation to it, not like allowing time to be on probation, yet be *in* time—the being that's possible for you to be living, operating, and standing in the space of possibility, knowing you have a commitment to time. The time is not against you or for you.

That's the romance of getting to be right about that moment.

Time is neither bad nor good. Time is. The closer you can experience time, the more you'll use time and time won't use you. You won't be a subject to the romantic sensation about time or what you wish time were or want time to be or what you need time to be or how time is not on your side. We can be with time.

You have time conquered when you use time and time doesn't use you.

The Dogma of Time

"Time and space are not conditions of existence, time and space is a model for thinking. Time is an illusion"
Albert Einstein

Einstein's dogma is an unquestioned belief. What's the number one dogma in the world? It's universal everywhere in the world, and we're all under the same dogma. Well, it's the day of the week. For example, "What day is today?" Is it Tuesday? Is it Wednesday? Let's say it's Tuesday. How do you know it's Tuesday? If it's January 31, how do you know it's January 31? There's no real concept of what day it is, so it's an unquestioned dogma.

When you look at it, and you question it, the day of the week doesn't reflect anything real, and time also doesn't exist in its real form. *Now* is the only moment that *is*. *It's now*. When you're in the moment of now, then the contract of your future and your past doesn't control what you're doing. You're truly out of the jar when you're in the moment. When you're not thinking about the future nor the past, you're truly living in the moment, and you're coming from that place in the moment.

Now is the only moment that is. It's now.

I know it sounds tricky, yet this isn't a "be here now" conversation. It's impossible to be anywhere else yet here and now. The idea is that you are in the most powerful state when you're present. This is, in a lot of ways, as a cure for aging.

There are different dogmas, understandings, or beliefs about how we're supposed to behave, act, feel at a certain age. Dogma of age dictates a people's life behavior and their emotional states for what they should have, should do, can do and more. Our bodies deteriorate or age differently. Your age is a completely fictional idea. The matrix about how we evolve, like what year or how old are you, is very individualized. There's no real reference point to how old you are. We're confined to the beliefs, understandings, and cultures that we're born into when we identify ourselves with a day, time, and a year that we are. If you want to break free of the dogma, first acknowledge that it is a dogma; that, for instance, what day of the week it is—whether it's Tuesday—is just something we agree on. What time it is, how old you are, are agreements we make with each other. There's nothing that guarantees that. You cannot prove that any given day is Tuesday except by what we agree on.

I know for a lot of people this will be hard to grasp, yet there's freedom and there's power, and there's control that you get by letting go of those dogmas.

Dream the Impossible

Like learning about the dogma of time to be *in* time, dreaming the impossible is to let go of the restraints that limit you in your normal thinking as well as your past and current thinking. By dreaming the impossible, you allow ourselves to have something that you couldn't have if you were looking at whether it was possible or not.

Dream the impossible, and then look for how to accomplish the dream. See how your collective ideas can produce that. You can take the impossible and create possibility from it and then find that you could accomplish it with the tools and people and that it is possible. Then you can start putting an action plan together. Starting from the place

Dream the impossible, seek the unknown and you will achieve greatness daily.

of dreaming the impossible, first of all, dreaming, so you allow yourself to be dreamy, and then impossibility gets rid of the restraint of your thinking. Dream the impossible, seek the unknown and you will achieve greatness daily. It's not impossible it just hasn't been done yet. I'll tell you again: dream the impossible.

CHAPTER 55

The Hardest Thing You Ever Do

You can't change what you refuse to confront. I'm going to tell you about the hardest thing you'll ever have to do in your entire life—the most difficult, the most challenging, the most impossible thing you'll ever have to deal with, the most painful, the most struggling, something that can take your breath away and upset you to the deep places of your soul. What am I talking about?

I am talking about openly confronting your possibility; it's the hardest thing you'll ever do. The start of the process is to sit on the idea that it's possible that you don't hear what you hear. That it's possible that you don't see what you see. That it's possible, you don't feel what you feel. That it's possible, you don't experience what you experience.

Consider that it's possible that you're wrong. Maybe it's possible that your life isn't working. That it is possible, you're not getting what you want. Maybe it's possible that you're not where you want to be.

I am talking about openly confronting your possibility; it's the hardest thing you'll ever do.

Or maybe it's possible that you have what you want. Maybe it's possible to be okay with who you are. Maybe it's possible that you don't need anything. Maybe it's possible that nothing is impossible. Maybe it's possible that "nothing is impossible" doesn't mean what you think it means. Maybe, it's possible what you believe isn't necessarily true, that what you think isn't necessarily real, that what you feel isn't necessarily what you feel, and you're not who you think you are.

That it's possible that I'm not—fill in the blank. That it's possible—whatever your complaint is, fill it in. That it's possible that I'm not unhappy. That it's possible that I'm not poor.

See all of these things will be questions by the time you get through this, because the hardest thing to confront is your possibilities. It takes courage, responsibility, dependability, and relentless and unwavering commitment to confronting a possibility. I'm saying that the hardest thing in life is going to be for you to confront the possibility. *What's possible for my life?* That's living at risk. That's living in the question of being open to what could happen, to being able to say yes to your possibility.

Some people have rules about what they can have and when they can have it. I say it's possible that you can be a rule maker or a rule breaker and have what you have whenever you choose to have it without following some predefined rule. Otherwise, you won't appreciate it. I challenge you: do you have what it takes to confront your possibility?

I'm on a quest to help people find what's possible for their lives. I search for people who are open to their possibilities

Challenge to Philosophy of Possibility

The Philosophy of Possibility struggle is to overcome in our minds precisely the belief system located in the left hemisphere of the brain, which is our model of the world. It is the paradigm that we use to carve and formulate the model that helps us navigate the world, and that we desperately fight to make right and defend at all costs. Ninety percent of the context of this is developed by age seven.

We also have the right hemisphere of our brain, which is the devil's advocate that challenges the model on a constant basis. The right hemisphere will undermine your model of the world you have depended on for the strength of your belief system, and how grounded you are in those beliefs. The right side of the brain is referenced as our creative side.

The toughest thing about the Philosophy of Possibility is that its realm exists above the right and left hemisphere. It's in a space where your right or left hemisphere does not have you. Where you can look at the model and world that you have, the paradigm and the belief system that you are operating from, and be able to see whether everything works for you. You are undermining every single possible thing that you've done right in your life, or that your belief system says right, to the point where you completely succumb to the devil's advocate that challenges your model of the world. There has to be a healthy balance between left and right hemisphere. Do not give one priority over the other. Have the superior awareness to hear both. You're able to watch your model of the world and the challenges to that model and be able to be above both.

You sit in the vast infinite emptiness and the nothingness and the meaninglessness of the space to allow all of the possibilities to enter your space.

When you have your belief system, and you have your devil's advocate left and right hemisphere, you're able to reach in and look at what's workable. Because ultimately, the Philosophy of Possibility is allowing everything to flow in, to find the most optimal and workable solution so that you open yourself to all the possibilities infinitely. You're not

limiting yourself to the options that could have you, yet opening an expanding universe of possibility that exists outside of
the realm of what you know, outside of what you know that you
don't know. You sit in the vast infinite emptiness and the nothingness and the meaninglessness of the space to allow all of the
possibilities to enter your space. Ultimately, that's what you're
looking to accomplish, and that is the essence of the Philosophy
of Possibility.

Part Five

YOUR TURN

CHAPTER 56

Now What to Do

*"We cannot solve our problems with the same thinking we used
when we created them."*
—*Albert Einstein*

I guide you through your experience in such a way that you get
something from nothing. From ridding yourselves of the options in your jar to get to the point of nothing and being nothing. Then, starting from *nothing,* you create what is something
in essence, which becomes *everything.*

That's essentially how the progress of change will begin without opinions, belief systems, and concepts. Only truth, openness, vulnerability, and experiencing of every moment without
manipulating, lying, twisting will guide ourselves through your
own experience so we're experiencing in a way that has a loose
mindset—an ability to take a look at what it may be, to give yourself enough space to see more than one viewpoint and what may
be causing your synthetic experience. Where is meaning coming
from projecting the ideas? What experience did you have that
projects that belief, concept, or twisted manipulation that may
not be working for you, that's confining you to the jar you're in?

You can look at our experience and allow for the space to be there. You can have an experience that can transform you from where you are, to who you need to be to do what you want to do so that you can have what you want to have. That's the process.

The Rest of the Journey

Living in possibility is a daily choice. It's your choice. In the beginning, it is not always easy, yet it will become easier. After a while, you won't have to remember or try. It becomes your way of being. Results are. Success is. Experience is. Justice is what it is. You are not your name. You are not your family. You are not your city. You are not your state. You are not your country. You are not your body. You are not your religion. You are not what you believe. You are not what you've read. You are not what you think. You are not your circumstances. "Try" does not exist. Hope does not exist. "Kind of" does not exist. "Maybe" does not exist. You are not the relationship you're in. Time doesn't exist. You are not. You are devoid of meaning. You are emptiness. You are meaningless. You are valueless, hopeless, and you are worthless.

When you understand and embrace that you are ageless, nameless, timeless, cultureless, family-less, hopeless, worthless, valueless, meaningless, and your life is pointless with no purpose—then you will truly be free. Before that, you had to evaluate, justify, reason, come up with stories to establish your worth, value, age, culture, name, family to institute your meaning in the world. You were constantly struggling and evaluating and positioning your meaning with objectives for reasons to justify, and those validations left you wanting and chasing endlessly.

You are meaningless. You are valueless, hopeless, and you are worthless.

If you realize the meaningless, hopeless, worthless essence of life, then you can embrace joy, freedom, and possibility that exists in life so that you can be completely free of slavery, that you have freedom which is power—the power of freedom, that guiding freedom and the avoidance of force—force that will put you in slavery. When you have to use force on other people, you're using slave tactics. When you use power, you free people and enlighten people from the misery of meaning, value, and hope. Once you release yourself from that, then you can truly embrace hope because you lean in into it. It doesn't own you. You can own hope. You can place hope, be hope, do hope. You have the freedom to place worth on what it is that you feel worthy of putting worth on and value. You have the power to add the meaning rather than meaning having the force on you.

When you understand and embrace that you are ageless, nameless, timeless, cultureless, family-less, hopeless, worthless, valueless, meaningless, and your life is pointless with no purpose—then you will truly be free.

When you realize that everyone is putting meaning on things, you can choose into that or choose out of it, yet you're not obligated to the options that are given to you. You have the freedom to choose, yet not from the force of guilt, fear, and obligation. Freedom is uplifting, choosing, embracing, absorbing, becoming, enlightening, and doing. That's power.

Force is doing it from the position not of love but from a place of have to, duty, obligation, and guilt. When you operate from love you do it with joy and fruits that are observable. You can pour yourself—your heart into it when you have that position. Then you'll shine like the most majestic architecture in history during the freest of time in economic strength rather than the force of economic desperation, control, and mass manipulation that built jars.

You can see the difference between when you're governed and guided in the light of power, which is, in my mind, the essence of going towards God. It's letting God guide you. When you're forced, your back is against God, and you don't see the fruits. You see misery, upset, anger, frustration, and betrayal under force. That's what you get when you operate in obligation and duty in a fearful way through control.

You have the power to add the meaning rather than meaning having the force on you.

Remember that control can have different levels. You have good control and bad control. Good control is like driving a car and having a steering wheel. Bad control would be to try and steer the car with the rear-view mirror. What if you have never seen a car in your life? What would the car be to you? Would you know how to steer your car? You have to understand where the steering wheel, gas pedal, and brake is and where the lights are when it gets dark. You may put the brakes on when you want to go. What's going to happen? Nothing right.

How do you unleash the possibility in you? How do you press the gas pedal and unleash that possibility, that freedom without being constrained by meaning or obligation or guilt or worthiness whether they're worthy or not? That's the position of going toward saying that you are worthless. Because then the concentration isn't whether you're worthy or not; it's that you're worthless—meaning that it isn't about your worth at all, neither having worth nor not having worth. It's that place of meaninglessness, that place of nothingness that place of the void that sucks in all possibility and gives you all the available possibilities without limiting your options.

That's the essence of worthlessness—to be worthless.

You're not trying to be worth something or to invalidate yourself and tell people you're not worth anything. If you can stand in the space of being worthless, meaningless, then you can get things done effortlessly, because you don't have to build a case based on reason, justification, and understanding and get people to fall in line with their different viewpoints so they match up to the viewpoints that you share so you can get them to do something. You don't have to do that. Trust yourself to let go and do from space that needs no validation.

You can simply, effortlessly, meaninglessly, worthlessly, without reason, and without justification do something. When you follow your true power, and you know inherently what is and what isn't, what works and what doesn't, then it isn't about being right or wrong. It's what works, and you do it with the goodness and love of your heart. You're open and full of life and possibility, free of the restraints, the traps that capture you, such as meaning and justification. These concepts will suck the power out of you because of your fear making you come up with all these concepts to handle your fears. Next, you get other people to get on board to excuse or exhaust them into a sort of hypnotic trance to get them to be okay with whatever it is. People are so tired of listening to justifications, reasons, excuses for something that's so simple to do.

I'm telling you today that possibility realizes that you can stand in that space, and you don't have to justify your existence by trying to create worth, purpose, and value. If someone tells you "you have to." Who are they to say that? You do not need to explain your actions. They were your actions. They're the past, and you're not your past, and it doesn't dictate your future. You can simply acknowledge what those actions are and go "Okay. That didn't work." And choose something different. You don't have to feel bad nor feel guilty about that. You don't have to live in that space, hell, misery, worry that you might do it again. No, you don't have to live there. You can live in space, create your meaning, worth, value, possibilities, and have the power and the freedom to make it happen.

Rather than asking for permission, see what and who is going to stop you. If your intentions are pure, good, and worthy, you'll be surprised at what you can accomplish. Many leaders hand out their restraints, codes, rules, and every obstacle because they're afraid that if you had the tools, you'll wreck everything. That you're too dumb to handle the responsibility and the accountability. However, the majority of people have the possibility in them and can be trusted to be committed, honest, responsible and accountable.

You can live in space, create your meaning, worth, value, possibilities, and have the power and the freedom to make it happen.

Yes, there are a few people that are physically or mentally challenged, yet, for the most part, you can do much more. You can take more care of more people and open up the production lines and possibilities to be able to see things as they are and create the life that is possible for you. You haven't even gotten started. These things have been around for hundreds and thousands of years, and people have put this out there.

Chapter 57

Moving Beyond Ourselves

In 2001, I had an abrupt event that came out of completely nowhere, causing an identity crisis that was almost fatal. In just six days I lost $15 million, my business and house, and was instantly $875,000 in debt, with no income, no job and living literally in my car while hiding it from BMW Financial Services. Everything I thought about myself—a powerful, respected employer of 33 employees, successful, happy, healthy, and wealthy—was completely gone.

I walked into the closet of the house that I had just lost, kneeled, placed into my mouth a 9mm gun, pulled back the trigger. I was completely ready to have lead travel through my mouth and out of the top of my skull releasing my body. The last of what I thought was left of my identity would be no more. A millionaire once before was no more. Then the image of my mother crying over my dead body flashed to my mind: "You don't bury your children," she said. These words and image were real to me because it had been stained into my mind from when my mother crying said it to her sister while we lowered my cousin Johnny into the ground from a gunshot wound. I pulled the gun out of my mouth, fell to the ground crying profusely, deeper than ever before. The idea that I had to start over was overwhelmingly agonizing. I was completely committed in that moment to ending my physical existence. This started me on the path of the questions and questioning the question that opened up my life. It's irreversibility profoundly impacting everything from the nothing. From this space, I understood the space of possibility that I had been driving my predominant thoughts to proceed forward and help as many people as possible.

So, you *can* live in possibility. You *do* live in possibility. You're already living in possibility. You're just looking at it from the options, you think are available for you. Think of it this way: it's like wearing blinders and looking backward. You live in possibility, yet you're running the race looking back at your history while life is happening, and you're concentrated on justifying what you might have been in the past so that you can somehow equalize it in your mind before you can move forward. You are already moving forward. Now is the time. This is the present. You're living in the possibility even if you don't acknowledge that you're living in possibility. Options are your choice. If you choose to let your name control you, then it will. If you choose to let your heritage limit or control your options, then you live in options. If you let your past dictate the options that are available in the future, then you live in those options, even though they are options you're creating. You're still in the possibility. You think, therefore you are because that's what you'll create.

You'll create in the space of your options, without even looking at your possibilities, because the only available options for you are the ones that are locked up in the identity of yourself: your name, your family, your neighborhood, your culture, your country, your religion, your bank account, your car, your home, the identity of the world and how you see it, the identity of God and how and what you think God is, and the identity of the stories that have been put on you that limit your options. Opening yourself up to the possibilities is like a new period, that's like no other time ever then right now.

By looking at something in a new light and opening it up to the possibility that you could see things in new ways. That new ideas and concepts you might not have heard before, you can completely see them through new eyes today, differently than you saw them before. You can add more viewpoints, understandings, a lot of dimensions to your life.

Life can be really interesting because what you think is minute and small can have a whole history behind it, the floor that you walk on has a whole history of it—where it came from, how who and why they got it there, who blessed it as far as making it something that we thought that we would want. There's a whole story behind everything that you see around you and limitless possibilities in every direction, that just by looking into it, you can find that you're not the options that you think your life is constrained to. You are unlimited and infinite possibility, and nothing. It's all available to you.

When you operate from the space of nothingness and infinite possibility, opening yourself up to letting in the floodgates of transcendence, then you can accept that you have the possibility and no possibility at the same time. Now we have transcended, and all can come to your personal universe, understanding, and identity or whatever you want to call it. You can duplicate these concepts and ideas, opening up this theory and basing it on these laws that you can open up your world to what is possible, free from possibility and open to the possibilities, yet not limited to the options, traps, constraints, and restraints that surround you in culture and life.

> **You are unlimited and infinite possibility, and nothing. It's all available to you.**

CHAPTER 58

The Struggle for Meaning

One of the biggest human battles is the struggle to have things, events, and experiences mean something. There's got to be a point to all this, a purpose. This can't all be for nothing, and what's happened, to me, my father, my country, etc. has to be for a reason, right?

Wrong! The meaning you attach to life and events causes mental and emotional suffering. You work hard to support your justification, stories, and reasons that explain the meaning of your life, yet it's completely untrue. You know it, other people know it, and you're not fooling anyone. This struggle takes you out of the moment and has you safely reliving the past, not experiencing the moment. It keeps you uncommitted to the moment, so you're not at risk.

Maybe it doesn't mean anything. Maybe it's not bad that it doesn't mean anything. Maybe it's okay that it is what it is, and that's all it is and all it ever will be. Meaning is the trap, and most of you are stuck with it. Possibility, no possibility, and transcendence

Wrong! The meaning you attach to life and events causes mental and emotional suffering.

are the detachment from meaning. Just consider the possibility that there is no meaning to life and no point. That life is meaningless and pointless. How much would you have to give up to even get to this as a possibility? My relationship, career, family, religion, personality, friendship—put in whatever you have to give up to truly be free of meaning. Instead, you cling to the idea that you can have a thought or a feeling, and it's got to mean something. You can't even be hungry without that saying something about you. Meaning is the constant for the human struggle for being.

Start an open dialogue with yourself and let it flow and flow to expose what's there not to get an answer, be with yourself and your conversation.

Instead, start with an internal stream of free-flowing with no point, meaning or purpose a conversation that goes from one random idea to next that could begin something like: What I'm experiencing now is anxiety, it's unclear to me, now I am looking to attach to any story, justification, reason, or whatever logic I can come up with to create meaning so that I can be right. I have an unclear internal struggle that I feel, almost like fear. I've been talked to by people who gave me a bunch of information that at the core of the message appeared like its true underlining message was really meant to correct what they viewed as my incorrect behavior. Interesting! They are trying to redirect what they think is my incorrect behavior—which I think had an element of domination to make me wrong. It appeared to prevent me from moving forward. I got trapped struggling to defend my actions, to justify my behavior, and to give stories that support my actions for things that I can't even change, that have already happened. I feel a need to nullify their attacks on me so that I can move forward and not be criticized and attacked in the future because I have ready-made justifications, stories, and excuses to defend my position. So that I'm not dominated or made to be wrong so I can be right. In essence, I want to survive and not succumb to the ideas that other people have about me. This internal struggle for meaning is really at the heart of it. All of that is something that already happened that is being used on me by others brought up in conversation to support whatever image or idea or belief they have about me." That was a random flow.

Start an open dialogue with yourself and let it flow and flow to expose what's there not to get an answer, be with yourself and your conversation.

CHAPTER 59

Beyond Ourselves Into the Zero State of Being

As you work on changing, progressing on the journey, you discover yourself transcending through your thoughts, feelings, and experiences. Transcendence through to the state of being at Zero. I am not looking to tell anybody how to be. Instead, allow yourself to transcend to your birth origin natural state of the authentic you in Zero state. Zero state is being that can be accomplished through the use and infinite vehicle used here which is by using the Philosophy of Possibility. So you can reach a heightened transcendence to Zero state, which you can "live in the question" transcended from possibilities, from everything that is in your life and everything that makes up and identifies and is you. Then you can transcend that to a higher state of Zero through the Philosophy of Possibility.

> **Zero is a grounded state of true freedom where you can be and allow anything and any moment, nothing, and no moment and everything is open to you.**

You get to a space where you transcend, being grounded in a state of Zero, which is a free state—a state of being open to all possibilities and also no possibility from Ground Zero. That space that even allows you just to let go of the Philosophy of Possibility. It is a state that you can get to, an elusive state of Zero being, a true transcendence that you can get there with the Philosophy of Possibility. Zero is a grounded state of true freedom where you can *be* and allow anything and any moment, nothing, and no moment and everything is open to you. Not just the Philosophy of Possibility, yet it includes everything at your disposal that's still in the domain of possibility, which you can bring in. The Philosophy of Possibility doesn't exclude. It uses nothing, everything, to get to the state that you want to get to, whatever that state may be—that you find your version of what I've called transcendence to the state of Zero. You can call it freedom. You can call it anything you like. You can call it enlightened. You can call it whatever you decide to call it, yet that space where you think completely often, to see, hear, think, feel, and not feel and not think and not see and not hear and be detached and unattached.

This Zero state of being is the purest form of authentic being that has "ABSOLUTE BLISS AND PEACE in being."

In meditative practices, this is the state of "no thoughts, no emotion"; of not being detached or attached to thought, emotion, physical body or thinking. In Hindu Yogic practices, it's a state of "pause" when we finished inhaling and were ready to exhale or exhale and are about to inhale.

This Zero state of being is the purest form of authentic being that has "ABSOLUTE BLISS AND PEACE in being." You become a true vessel vacuum or emptiness truly open in the state of Zero. This point in being has an infinite number of axes and is truly the strongest platform to being anything and everything. No value has all value in this space. In science, it has a very special value. It is the mid-point of number axis at the jump off point where an infinite number ax comes to an "end" and the numbers "change" their value.

Achieving Transcendence Through Possibility to the State of Zero

"I think 99 times and find nothing. I stop thinking, swim in silence, and the truth comes to me." ~Albert Einstein.

The goal is the state of Zero completing your transcendence, existential transcendence, being freed from your existence, your thinking existence, your feeling existence, and your body's existence. It's like an out-of-body, out-of-mind space where, yes, you use a body, mind, and everything that is disposable in possibility, yet you transcend the limitations of all those instruments. You move past your existent belief of what limitations you have about your possibilities, and you open the question and transcend into the space where all things are possible, and nothing is out of reach. From here you have reached the authentic state of Zero.

That's the space of possibility and state of Zero. It's anything that you can work on and discover that will work on bringing out the possibilities that are there, transcendence to the state of Zero. You use the Philosophy of Possibility because that's the greatest way to get at opening the door to the state of Zero. When you look at life from true possibility, from the idea that you don't know what you don't know, that's possibility. You don't know what you don't know about limitations. You don't know what you don't know about what's keeping you from who you want to be, what you want to do or what you'd like to have. It's getting through the process of transcendence into the state of Zero so you can in space of possibility project and generate yourself, project yourself into the future, project yourself into the past, and be in the moment, so that we can see, hear things maybe for the first time—the freeing powerful space possibility and the state of Zero.

This transcendent past, what you hear today, what you've heard before, and what you're trying to hear coming close to what is being said, not said, and all the parts of it. Transcendence through possibility is the technology, the tool you use to get where you want to be. The possibility is the philosophy. The philosophy is designed with the goal of existential transcendence "free of existence" to the state of Zero. To take the meaningless and nothingness of life, transcend that, and generate what it is that you like, want, whatever it may be, that you can become, you can do, you can have what it is that you want without the barriers, rules, and limitations. Of course, not carelessly and not breaking the law because that would be not being responsible, yet transcending limitations, to transcend past the physical, emotional, mental, and conceptual ideas that you have about yourselves, your friends, your countries, your neighborhoods, our animals, your food.

You can transcend past whatever concepts or rules or past experiences that you have that dictate our current moment.

> The philosophy is designed with the goal of existential transcendence "free of existence" to the state of Zero.

That tell you or feed you with the information that can often be inaccurate misinformation, mis-emotion, and mis-physical feelings, not necessarily true or real.

You're not necessarily connected to your emotions. You're not necessarily connected to your thoughts. You're not necessarily even connected to your body. You're not necessarily connected to your past. You're not necessarily connected to your friends. You're not necessarily connected to your family. Now your body may be similar to nature, cells, and DNA. You may be connected in that way to your family.

You that is you, not the body that your parents gave the

name to, not that part of you, but you that is here, maybe before and maybe a bit of the energy that keeps that body alive. The possible essence that is connected to maybe all four things, and maybe it's connected to nothing when you look at it from an all-encompassing goal through the transcended state of Zero.

You've even transcended any possibility of the "right or wrong" conversation. It isn't about right or wrong anymore. It's about what works and what doesn't. If it works, how good does it work? Do you want it to work that way? Could it work some other way? What's possible in that space as far as making it work? Can we automate that? Do we want to automate that? Do we enjoy the craftiness of doing it by hand and that produces a more meaningful or spiritual meaning to it?

That's the transcendences to Zero. You don't have a fixed idea of what something should or shouldn't be, would or wouldn't be. You've transcended that conversation. You've transcended where you are and are open to the possibilities from that Zero state.

What helps you transcend is the use of the Philosophy of Possibility; they are intertwined, and possibility helps you transcend your mind, your bodies, and your thoughts by looking and noticing your limitations. That's all. Just simply looking. Turning the lights on in that area. Just simply listening in that area. When you listen and open space, you may notice that you hear things you haven't heard before. You may notice that there are things not being said and may be a purpose for why they are not being said and that it's possible that's there more to be heard in that space. You're open to the connectedness of when you hear too many other things, whether they're different, and you identify with them, or you associate with them, or you can see the differentiation between one thing and another.

When you transcend your identification, you have the flexibility to see things in a different way—things that you identified with. With new information, you can get to a place where you can say, "Wow, I see how that has changed." You can take something that you have identified with, and as you notice new information, it can easily change.

The meaning can change for you. You have the complete flexibility to identify or not with things in a new way. To associate with things in a completely new way, a way just by noticing a new perspective and gathering new information, you can allow the ability to where if you see something that associates with something, you can have it, and if you don't, you can let it go. You can let go of the idea that it was ever associated. You have complete flexibility when you transcend that space of being, able to identify, associate, and ultimately differentiate from things, the difference from one thing to another. With new information, you can identify, you can associate, and you can differentiate something, different because you have new information where you may have identified it in an associated group. Now, you can differentiate it from the group.

When you look at transcendent past, you that might have been before, that may be after, the energy that gives you the essence of being alive, the essence of you, you are in a space where no possibility exists.

The true goal of possibility is to get to a place where there is no possibility. To get to a place where there is absolutely no possibility, no "thing." There is no possibility. When you can transcend the space of possibility and go and "be in a question," then you've transcended possibility to a place where you can have the possibility or not have the possibility, to be free of possibility at zero. The Philosophy of Possibility is setting you free, to transcend in your existence, to be in space and in the question where life can reach you, and you have the ability to reach life.

If you can reach it, you can have it. As much as you can

be responsible for you will have. Whatever you can reach you can have! That's the key to transcendence. When you reach Zero state, you can have anything, everything, and nothing. You completely have the flexibility to be, do and have because you've transcended all the aspects and barriers to being free, to being, doing, and having what you want.

When you transcend to Zero, and you are where you don't have to trust yourself anymore, and you don't have not to trust yourself anymore, that you can just be without trying not to be something and not trying to be something, you transcend, and you *are*. When you're in the space of are and is, and you are in the space of *who,* not "am I" or "I am," when you get the

If you can reach it, you can have it. As much as you can be responsible for you will have.

past and let go of "I am," then you're in the essence the freedom of Zero which the Philosophy of Possibility has the hope for creating your transcendent authentic Zero self. You're free to experience Now the ultimate power of Zero! This is power to access the infinite intelligence of the universe.

From the state of Zero you get the power to access INFINITE INTELLIGENCE. Einstein focused on empting his mind to access this intelligence to create, imagine, and invent the Theory of Relativity. Thomas Edison emptied from his mind of the options and rules of what was possible and tried 9,999 failed attempts to create the first light bulb on the 10,000 attempt. Walt Disney emptied his mind to allow his imagination to run free, to create and let flow out this infinite intelligence into the world. Steve Jobs' desire for beauty, intuition and perfection emptied out the known, the impossible and the

You're free to experience Now the ultimate power of Zero!

options to access infinite intelligence and his actions affected four industries creating the biggest publicly traded company in the world. THIS INFINITE INTELLIGENCE IS IN ALL OF US, FROM THE STATE OF ZERO WE GET ACCESS TO THE UNKNOWN-UNKNOWN FROM THERE YOU CAN KNOW THE POSSIBLE AND CREATE OPPORTUNITY!

THE LAWS OF POSSIBILITY

The State of Zero

1. You are not who you think you are.
2. You are not what you feel you are.
3. You are not your body.
4. You are not your name.
5. You are not your family.
6. You are not where you come from.
7. You are not your emotions.
8. You are not your past.
9. You are not your future.
10. You are what you are.
11. Everything is as it is.
12. Nothing is as it is.
13. Because does not exist.
14. Reason does not exist.
15. Excuses do not exist.
16. Justification does not exist.
17. Stories do not exist.
18. There is no beginning
19. There is no end
20. Time does not exist.

Anna Zakowska, Andrew Cartwright, John Travolta and Kelly Preston out for a dinner on the town in Las Vegas at the Wynn Casino.

Andrew and Rami Malek, Star of Mr Robot.

Bill Bellamy and Andrew having fun and
raising awareness and funds for a cause.

Andrew and Mark Cuban.

Renee Zellweger and Andrew at Palace of Fine Arts in San Francisco.

Cuba Gooding Jr and Andrew in the movie "What Dreams May Come" on
the set in Vallejo California; a scene in Hell.

Robin Williams and Andrew after 18 hours on the set of "What Dreams May Come" in Vallejo California; in a scene in Hell.

30,000 sq. ft. Very unique 11 dock, 1 grade level doors. Logistics building, one of the many developments completed by Andrew, from dirt to finish.

Commercial subdivision and shipping building under construction.

Jay Leno and Andrew on backlot of
Universal Studios Hollywood before Jay's show.

Good friends Jonathon Scott of the Property Brothers shows, Andrew, and The Amazing Johnathan headline on the Las Vegas strip and pioneer of Magic Comedy. Very talented artists.

George Lucas creator of Star Wars, Industrial Lights and Magic and so much more, and Andrew out for dinner in San Francisco.

30K building
7 Commercial Sub-Division
626 St Croix, 519 Regents Gate Interior of 508

Completed from dirt, design and to finish. Top left 626 St Croix 8,562 sqft
5 Bed 7 Bath Sold in 2014 for $4,575,000. Estimated 2017 at $5,476,138.
Top right 519 Regents Gate 7,341 sqft 6 beds 8 baths. Bottom is 508
Regents Gate 11,060 6 beds 8 baths celebrity house featured on A & E
Flipping Vegas season finally Dream home episode. Also Andrew built
next store 512 Regents Gate 6,331 Sqft 4 beds 7 baths.

Good friends Wade Martin DJ, artist, and music producer (Will.i.am, Britney Spears, Rolling Stones, 50 cent, DMX, Steve Aoki, many more), Andrew, and John Payne, musician known for being Asia lead singer.

Steve Aoki, Andrew, and Anna.

Anna, Rick Harrison of Pawn Stars, and Andrew.

Cheech Marin and Andrew.

About the Author

Born and raised in Northern California, Andrew Cartwright has been an entrepreneur since the age of twelve. By seventeen, he had locked down exclusive rights for Northern California on a candy line that would make him a millionaire. He soon opened several offices, other companies, and expanded into manufacturing. By age twenty-six Andrew retired to pursue his dream of acting and joined the exclusive union of the Screen Actors Guild. He spent three years acting in several movies, commercials, and theater and was the international face for Microsoft Office 2000. His acting credits include working with Robin Williams, Philip Seymour Hoffman, Cuba Gooding Jr, Renée Zellweger, Cheech Marin, Don Johnson, James Cromwell, and Clint Eastwood, as well as starring in an A&E television network series as a real estate developer. In 1999, he moved to Las Vegas to open several companies. Today, Andrew has successfully opened and run companies in seventeen different industries. He has also developed, constructed, and sold residential and commercial projects, while purchasing, selling, and managing various real estate projects while coaching and consulting.

Andrew has become a self-made multimillionaire entrepreneur three separate times. He defines his entrepreneurial lifestyle this way: "a rebel thinker who broke reality three different times with his success blueprint for thinking by creating something from nothing." He continues to enjoy challenging fixed ideas, unconscious beliefs, and debunking limitations to open up opportunities for people around the world.

For more information, contact Andrew at:

www.andrewcartwright.com

or

www.OriginofOpportunity.com